THE BLESSI

THE
BLESSING
THIS IS YOUR TIME!

JIM CERNERO

The Blessing: This Is Your Time!

ISBN: 978-1-943730-02-5

Published by:
Jim Cernero/Certain Sound Ministries
Round Rock, Texas USA

JimCernero.org
Facebook.com/JimCernero
Twitter: @JimCernero

Cover Photography: Daniel Cernero
Cover Design: Stephanie Palmquist
Editor: Sheryl Palmquist

Produced in the United States of America.

DEDICATION

This book is dedicated to my wife of thirty years, Mindy. Your love, commitment and devotion have been a source of strength and comfort to me. I praise God for bringing us together and for the journey He has allowed us to take these past thirty years. You have been a wonderful mother to our son, Daniel also. You, Daniel and now his wife, our beautiful daughter-in-love, Linsey are precious treasures of my heart.

TRIBUTE

To my precious Mom: You are no longer here on earth with us but your presence in my heart and the impact of your life of faith in Christ and love of the Lord will never fade from my memory. Your love for the Word, your trust in the Word, your unwavering faith in the Word of God, helped to shape me into the man I have become and the minister I now am. You are the exemplification of the truth of this book: The Blessing: This is Your Time! You often would say, "Pray in the Spirit, Jim" when going through a difficult challenge, and that invaluable council has brought me to an awareness of the of the Holy Spirit's presence and power and brought me victoriously through many tough circumstances. Until I see you in heaven, rest in the fact that your life well-lived has not only touched your sons' lives, their families and our immediate family, but is touching many as we continue on in your legacy of faith and preach the gospel around the world.   I love you, Mom.

RACHEL ANNE CERNERO (1926 – 2013)

To my Dad: You left us 21 years ago now, but your rock solid faith in the Lord, consistent disposition of peace, and unshakable trust in God and His Word have left an indelible imprint on your four sons and their families. Thank you for being the hard worker, provider and Man of God that you were! In an age where integrity is sometimes in short supply, your godly character stands as a testament to Jesus Christ, whom you lived for all of your 71 years here on earth. You prayed that the Lord would send your sons "to the four corners of the earth" and God certainly heard your prayer, Dad! I love you, Dad.

NUNZIANTE CERNERO (1923 - 1994)

To my eldest brother, Tom: It still seems hard to fathom that you are no longer with us also! Your life, while a short 64 years, was none-the-less a sweet testament of your faith in Christ, love of family and country. Your tremendous wit, fantastic sense of humor, ability to communicate, kindness, integrity and desire to serve others was exemplary. Your selfless devotion to Mom and Dad in caring for them in the latter years of their lives was not only model for all, but enabled me and our brothers, Mark and John, to serve in ministry and fulfill the call of God on our lives. You were the one to put up the money for my first missions trip to Africa in 1975; the beginning of my world wide ministry! You were a treasured brother and friend. Much love, Tom.

THOMAS NUNZIO CERNERO (1949 – 2013)

ENDORSEMENTS

Jim Cernero has proven, Spirit-led, faith-inspiring ministry and is well known for his personal integrity. He has been given great favor by God and is deeply respected as a revivalist, teacher, psalmist and healing evangelist within diverse streams of the church.

Every Christian desires to experience God's best for their lives, but so few, it seems, know how to get there. In *The Blessing,* Jim unpacks this often misunderstood topic with biblical clarity and dynamic personal insight. Jim shows us how walking in obedience opens the supernatural doors of the Blessing of Abraham for us today!

Tim Enloe, Author / Teacher
Holy Spirit Conferences

Jim Cernero's new book, *The Blessing: This Is Your Time* is a great read. It examines the Spirit-Empowered life we as believers are to live and the destiny this launches us into. It is an inspiration and impartation for our lives.

Robert Henderson, Pastor

In this insightful teaching James Cernero has tapped into a wonderful revelation of God's redemptive plan of blessing as we realize that God's goodness is meant to not only flow from our lives but blessings are to overflow as we open our hearts to God's purpose of spreading His goodness through the world. This book is a don't miss read.

Kent Mattox, Senior Pastor
Word Alive International Outreach, Oxford, Al

CONTENTS

Foreword

Introduction

Chapter 1	Recognizing the Blessing	25
Chapter 2	This Is Your Time!	43
Chapter 3	The Blessing of Grace	59
Chapter 4	The Blessing of Salvation and Righteousness	75
Chapter 5	The Blessing of Health and Healing	93
Chapter 6	The Blessing of Peace... The Shalom Blessing	113
Chapter 7	The Blessing of a Godly Heritage of Faith	129
Chapter 8	The Blessing of Faith to Believe for the Impossible	147
Chapter 9	The Blessing of Abundance	165
Chapter 10	The Blessing of Supernatural Intervention and the Miraculous	185
Chapter 11	The Blessing of Restoration and Recovery	201
Chapter 12	The Blessing of Divine Protection	219
Chapter 13	The Blessing of "Another" or a Different Spirit	237
Chapter 14	The Blessing of a Heart Transplant and the Promise of Ezekiel 36	257
Chapter 15	I Just Want Breath to Praise Him	275
Chapter 16	Receiving and Releasing the Blessing	287

FOREWORD

Few things are more thrilling than when Jim Cernero takes his place before a mass choir and leads them in worship music so familiar in our crusades, especially as the momentum builds. How many times over past decades have I seen the anointing fall on him, the choir, and our audiences. And when the refrain begins, "Then sings my soul, my Savior God, to Thee: How great Thou art! How great Thou art!" I can easily imagine how the heavenly choirs must sound!

Jim stood with me through our early crusades and was with me when I preached to record crowds of 7.4 million people (three services total) in India, and through it all, I have considered it an honor to work with this faithful man of God.

Yet there is so much more to this dear musician than our crusade crowds get to see. He is a powerful preacher, a remarkable Bible teacher, a wonderful family man, and one of my dearest friends in the world.

He is also a remarkable author, as you will see in *The Blessing*. It is somewhat autobiographical, beginning with the heart-pounding scene involving his ten-year-old twin brother and himself as they witness a life-and-death emergency involving their own mother. Throughout the book, he uses the principles God has taught him about blessings and tenacious faith.

In the first chapter, he writes very pointedly: there is nothing that you are going through that the breath of the Holy Spirit cannot change and transform! I have experienced it in my life on many occasions and seen situations change that once seemed absolutely impossible and insurmountable, and what was once dead, come back to life. If He did it for me, He can and will do it for you!

From that passage he builds precept upon precept of life-changing principles that will tug at your heartstrings and help build your faith.

Chapter 15 is one of my personal favorites. I won't give anything away, but "I Just Want Breath to Praise Him" includes how Jim and I ended up meeting and working together. The situation is "impossible" in the natural, but we know there was nothing impossible with God!

He has touched my life beyond measure, and I know this powerful book will touch your heart, too. May God bless you as you read the pages of *The Blessing*, and may God bless Jim Cernero as his ministry continues to grow and expand!

— BENNY HINN

INTRODUCTION

What would you say if you were approached by someone asking, "Would you like to be blessed or live a blessed life?" I'm quite certain that you would respond as the majority of people would with something like, "Absolutely!" It's inherently part of us to desire to be blessed whether we are conscious of it or not. In fact, that may have had some part in what attracted you to pick up this book and begin reading it. However, our perspective on what it really means to be blessed may differ.

When the word "blessed" is mentioned, one of the first things that comes to mind for most individuals is being blessed financially and having material blessings and wealth. We think of men like Donald Trump, Warren Buffet, and other wealthy business men and women like them and imagine how awesome it would be to be them. To others it would be the blessing of enjoying exceptional health. After all, what good is all the money in the world without health to enjoy it? To some it might be to have peace in one's life or peace of mind. How many wealthy individuals who live emotionally tumultuous lives would exchange their fortune for the priceless treasure of a moment's peace of mind?

What if you could have it all? That's my question to you today.

You might be thinking, "That's not possible, is it?" Actually, I happen to be one who believes it is! I believe it's possible to be blessed in every area of your life, including: physical health and strength to live a life of purpose and fulfillment, a family life that is healthy and happy, financial favor and abundance, and most importantly, to be at peace with God spiritually. Let's look at how you can live the blessed life that is available to you starting today!

CHAPTER ONE

Recognizing the Blessing

"John … I hear a siren! " I shouted to my twin brother. "Do you hear it? Sounds like it's coming this way …"

It was 1964 and my twin brother and I were 10 years old. We were playing with some neighborhood friends in a heavily wooded area behind our backyard … one of our favorite places to play after school. It was a carefree day and the piercing noise had interrupted our adventure so we stopped momentarily to listen. The sound was getting louder and louder, and it seemed to be getting closer by the moment. Curious to see what was happening, John and I ran back towards our house following the well-worn path through the woods up through our backyard with our friends following close behind.

As we ran around to the front of the house, imagine our surprise to see the flashing lights of an ambulance and a police squad car parked there … lights flashing and emergency personnel hurrying around! In the midst of all this noise and activity, we saw a stretcher carried by two uniformed men emerge from the front door, and our Mom was on the stretcher with an oxygen mask over her face! Mom had been sick with a severe case of bronchitis, but judging by all the activity and the sirens, her condition had worsened and something was drastically wrong!

An Unforgettable Look

John and I watched the frightening scene unfold before us like a movie in slow motion. Our father was away at work, and strangers were maneuvering the stretcher with our Mom on it in the direction of the ambulance. As the emergency personnel whisked her past us, it was impossible for her to speak to us because of the oxygen mask that covered her nose and mouth. However, I can still remember the look on Mom's face while trying to get enough air to breathe, not of fear but of concern for how we might be afraid of what was happening to her. As she struggled to breathe, her loving eyes were trying to assure us that everything would be okay. Mom was always taking care of others, and we had never seen her like this before. It was a frightening experience ... one of those things in your childhood that you never forget!

The ambulance doors closed and sped away, rushing our Mom to the nearest local hospital. We learned later that the medication prescribed to help treat my Mom's acute bronchitis caused a serious allergic reaction, which almost killed her. The prescription contained the drug codeine ... a drug that neither my mother or her doctor knew she was allergic to. She experienced an extremely negative reaction to the prescribed drug and went into complete anaphylactic shock, making it impossible for her to breathe. Thankfully, through the power of prayer and making the necessary adjustment in her medication, she survived the life-threatening incident and was back home in a few days taking care of her four boys and her husband. However, that experience was a traumatic one, leaving an impression on all of us as young children. It also left my Mom with ongoing breathing difficulties and a nagging chronic cough for the rest of her life. Even though she lived a fairly normal life for many years, her body was prone to recurring bronchitis and on many occasions, she found it difficult to breathe properly.

If you've ever had your breathing impaired or experienced any sudden difficulty in taking a breath, you know that it is a frightening experience. Breath is essential to life, and when that natural reflex is hindered in any way, terror strikes. Suddenly, you find yourself gasping for breath as fear grips you at the prospect of not being able to breathe.

Just as a person's regular intake of oxygen sustains life physically, the breath of the Spirit of God is essential for spiritual life. The human breath affects life down to the cellular level of an individual, oxygenating the blood and bringing life to every cell of the body. God's breath … the breath of the Spirit … has even more power … power to heal not only the soul, but the body, the mind, and affect every aspect of a person's life. The Bible refers to this spiritual breath as the Blessing of Abraham and this book will hopefully help you to come to an understanding of exactly what is included in that blessing and how you can experience it for yourself.

Blessed With Breath

The book of Genesis tells us that the Lord God breathed the breath of life into man at creation and man became a living soul. "And the Lord God formed man of the dust of the ground, and breathed into his nostrils the breath of life; and man became a living soul" (Gen. 2:7). Adam would have remained a lump of clay on the ground if God hadn't breathed the breath of life into his nostrils. He (God) has been breathing natural life into all those have been born on this planet since Adam and when one has a personal encounter with Him, He breathes spiritual life and power into that person bringing about spiritual birth, continuous breath of His Spirit eternally, and the possibility for miraculous things to happen in that person's life.

Abram, The Father of All Who Believe

Such was the case also with a man by the name of Abram in Scripture who became the Father of not only the Jewish people, but according to the New Testament of the Bible, is also the "Father of all them that believe" (Rom. 4:11) in Christ as their Savior. His story is recorded later in the book of Genesis, beginning at chapter 12. When God breathed into Abram, whose name meant in the Hebrew language "high father" or "exalted father," in chapter 17 of Genesis, a tremendous miracle occurred opening the way for everyone, including you and me, to be blessed beyond measure … abundantly, beyond our imagination.

You see, this man named Abram had an encounter with God's Holy Spirit and when he did, not only was his name changed to Abraham, but he was also transformed by that encounter in every way! From that moment on, his life was blessed in every dimension: spiritually, physically, financially and so on, so much so that the Bible describes it as The Blessing of Abraham (Gal.3:14). Even more importantly, it was passed down through the generations to his children, his children's children and most amazingly also to those, who though they are not his descendants by blood, yet have become eligible through faith in Jesus Christ, Abraham's seed, as their Lord and Savior. Stay with me as I establish for you just how and why you need to know about this blessing of Abraham and just how you can be a recipient of it today and every day of your life from now on!

God's Covenant of Blessing With Abraham

Imagine that you are this man who as I mentioned was originally named Abram and one day you're just going along par for the course, and suddenly you have a supernatural visitation from none other than the Lord God Himself. That alone would be enough excitement and a life-altering experience but on top of that, HE (God) speaks and says something amazing to you that your mind cannot even begin to conceive is possible because up until now, there is no evidence in your life to even give you a glimmer of hope that it will happen! Here's what God said to him. "Now the Lord had said to Abram: 'Get out of your country, From your family And from your father's house, To a land that I will show you. I will make you a great nation; I will bless you

And make your name great; And you shall be a blessing. I will bless those who bless you, And I will curse him who curses you; And in you all the families of the earth shall be blessed" (Gen. 12:1–3).

Abrams Believed And Obeyed

As amazing as this encounter with the Most High God was, what's even more amazing is that Abram believed what God told him and immediately obeyed God and did exactly what He said. He picked up lock, stock and barrel and left his home, his extended family, his livelihood, and his country and set out to find the land that God had spoken to him about. "So Abram departed, as the Lord had spoken unto him; and Lot went with him: and Abram was seventy and five years old when he departed out of Haran" (Gen. 12:4). Now that's faith! That act of faith was the key that began to unlock the blessing in his life and changed his destiny forever! Often an act of faith, a stepping out of your comfort zone and taking a risk is necessary for us to open the door to blessing and begin to realize God's abundant provision and promise.

I'm sure that Abram's family back in Haran must have thought he had lost is mind, probably saying, "You're going to do what, Abram? Leave your familiar surroundings, your country; your family, your religion, and go to a strange land that you know absolutely nothing about? You must have been in the sun a little too long, son!" However, Abraham, according to Romans 4:17 "believed in the God who calls [speaks into being] those things are not, as though they were."

As It Is In Heaven

God speaks over us "as it is in heaven," not as it is on earth. When He declares something about our destiny, our situation, our health, our life, He speaks from a greater reality than what our finite, limited minds can even conceive. He speaks from the timeless realm that He alone occupies. There may not be the slightest trace of evidence that what He has promised will happen but that doesn't change the fact that if God says it, then it will come to pass! "My Word shall not return unto me void but will accomplish that which I please and prosper in the things whereto I send it" (Isa. 55:11).

Furthermore, Jesus taught us to pray, "Our Father, who art in heaven, hallowed be Thy Name; Thy Kingdom come, Thy will be done, on earth… as it is in heaven" (Matt. 6:9-10). Did you catch that? He was saying, My will for you, My disciples, My followers, My children, children of Abraham, is that it would be for you on earth as it is in heaven. Have you ever asked yourself this question? Just how is it in heaven? Is there sickness and disease in heaven? Is there poverty or lack there? Is there strife and division there? Is there fear, oppression or bondage of any kind? Confusion? The obvious answer to these rhetorical questions is, NO! God wants us to experience the benefits of heaven right here on earth. It's only by faith that we can bring those benefits to earth when we listen to His Word, agree with it in our hearts, and act on the promises just as Abram did.

Something in this man Abram understood this truth and made him willing to stake his entire future on it, regardless of what anyone else thought. It propelled him into God's supernatural realm, and it was only a matter of time before he would receive the promise!

Never allow anyone, no matter how much you respect them nor how prominent they may be in your life, to define your destiny or limit you to what place they see you in or how far you can go. I'm not suggesting that we should not keep a spirit of humility for the Word of God tells us that we should respect those that God has put in authority over us and submit to their authority. I believe in all of those things. However, the Lord, our Ultimate authority said, "My sheep know my voice." When you have heard the voice of the Lord, waited on Him to confirm it with His Word and by other signs, then it is disobedience not to obey and step out into what He has called you to do, regardless of whether or not it meets the approval of those who feel they know better. Now let's pick back up where we left off on the story of what happened to this man Abram and see how God brought about the miraculous fulfillment of His promise to him.

God Always Keeps His Promise

Abram was 75 years old when God spoke to him and when he left his country in obedience to the divine directive he received. Now fast forward to when Abram is 99 years old (Gen. 17:1) and after 24 years of holding onto the promise that God made him and to the Word of the Lord, he has yet to experience the fulfillment of the promise. However, God appeared to him again and assured him He hadn't forgotten His promise. "And when Abram was ninety years old and nine, the Lord appeared to Abram, and said unto him, I am the Almighty God; walk before me, and be thou perfect. And

I will make my covenant between me and thee, and will multiply thee exceedingly" (Gen. 17:1-2).

Enlarged Territory

At the end of verse one, The Lord says to Abram, "Walk before Me and be thou perfect." When we come in contact with the Spirit of the Lord, the Almighty, we begin to walk in new territory. In this enlarged territory He perfects or makes whole every dimension of our lives … body, mind, soul and spirit. It is a realm of fullness that cannot be attained unto by any other means but by Him pouring Himself into us. And just as a branch receives its life and sustenance from the vine, so we receive divine life from Him. This word "perfect" not only means blameless but also complete or whole.

Very often God will allow us to come to the end of ourselves, our ability, and our resources so that the only thing we can do is to completely trust Him and lean on Him to bring about a supernatural miracle of divine supply and enabling.

You will notice in Genesis 17:1 that when Abram again has an encounter with the Lord, the El Shaddai, he is 99 years old and completely beyond the age reproductively to father a child. Suddenly, the finite meets the Infinite One, the deadness of his body in it's ability to reproduce meets the Living God, the giver of life; the earthly meets the Heavenly One; the natural meets the Supernatural and when that happened, Abram was suddenly connected to the miraculous, healing, creative power of the Almighty.

The Giver of Life

In fact, His Name "El Shaddai" is derived from the Hebrew word shad or breast. It is the connotation of a mother bringing her completely dependent child to her breast to satisfy the hunger and provide the nourishment needed for life to be sustained. The child would die apart from the nourishment from the mother and is totally dependent on her for life. So it was with the patriarch Abraham; prior to this life-altering visitation of the Most High, he was unable to produce a child. The moment He came in contact with Divine Supply, the El Shaddai quickened his body and supplied what only He could give … life. He is the Spirit of life.

In this amazing encounter with the Almighty, God reiterated His covenant of blessing that He made with Abram and changed his name from Abram, or exalted father to Abraham, or father of many nations. "And Abram fell on his face: and God talked with him, saying, As for me, behold, my covenant is with thee, and thou shalt be a father of many nations. **Neither shall thy name any more be called Abram, but thy name shall be Abraham; for a father of many nations have I made thee.** And I will make thee exceeding fruitful, and I will make nations of thee, and kings shall come out of thee. And I will establish my covenant between me and thee and thy seed after thee in their generations for an everlasting covenant, to be a God unto thee, and to thy seed after thee" (Gen. 17:3-8).

More Than A Name

Today, very often we choose a name for a baby that's about to be born because we like the name or the way the name sounds coupled with another name and surname, but not so in Biblical times. Names were very important. To have a name that didn't truly represent you was a problem. For example, it might have been a little embarrassing for Abram to be called "exalted father" but in actuality, he had no biological offspring! But you see, when God is about to do something extraordinary through you or in you, He will often "call" you, or "re-name" you according to how He sees you and not how others, as well-meaning as they may be, see you or perceive you. Your parents, as much as they may have loved you and desired the very best for you, might not have imagined what God has put in you. You might not even be aware of what potential is locked deep inside of you just waiting to be released. You may not recognize what talents God has placed in you that at present are lying dormant, but HE knows; He put them there in the first place and called them over your life long before you were born. You may not yet comprehend the full scope of what God wants to do through you and bring about in your life, but He does! A moment in His presence like Abram had and your eyes will open and you will discover His plan for your life and just how much He wants to bless you!

Miraculous grace was dispersed into Abram's body, so much so that it necessitated a name change as his very disposition and destiny were forever altered in that divine moment.

The Blessing of A Name Change

As I have made reference to already, originally, Abraham and Sarah's names were Abram and Sarai instead of the names that we have come to know them by. That is because these were their given names "before" God significantly and supernaturally blessed them and changed them in Genesis 17:5. You might be wondering, so what? What's the significance of their name change? What's the big deal? The answer is: it's a VERY big deal and when you understand, I believe you will agree! Let me explain why that is the case.

Something extraordinary happened as a result of the encounter he had with the El Shaddai in Genesis 17. Not only did the Lord reiterate His promise to him — the promise that he would have a son and that he would be the father of many nations — but He also changed his name. It is interesting to me that this is recorded in verse 5 of the chapter. You will understand why I said that in a few minutes as I continue to unpack this truth for you. You see, there are no meaningless details in the Word of God and if we will ask the Holy Spirit to reveal truth to us, He will open up the hidden treasures. In fact, right now, while you're reading this chapter, why not stop for a moment and ask the Holy Spirit to "open the eyes of your understanding" and reveal this truth to you? I promise you, if you do, He will do it for you.

Prayer:
"Holy Spirit, open the eyes of my understanding so that the hidden treasures in the Word of God will become life and substance to me. Transform me by this revelation of truth so that I can experience Your supernatural power like Father Abraham did. Amen!"

So here in Genesis 17:5, the Lord says to Abram, "Neither shall thy name any more be called Abram, but thy name be Abraham; for a father of nations have I made thee" (KJV).

God's Promises Are NOW Promises

Before I comment on the first part of this amazing declaration the Lord makes over Abram, let me draw your attention to the wording of the last phrase …. "for a father of nations have I made thee." Notice the tense here, have. In other words, it had already been accomplished. He didn't say I am about to make you, or I will eventually make you; the Hebrew word here translates to the English past tense, have. This is because it exists outside of time as we know it! When He speaks or calls things, He calls it the way He sees it or the way that it is in heaven. When our faith is quickened or made alive like Abram's was, we enter that timeless realm where God exists and miracles begin to happen!

You see, when the Lord speaks a promise over us, He speaks in a tense that is most true and accurate; He speaks as though it has already happened or been accomplished, because it has! In Matthew 12 (Matt. 12:13, Luke 6:10) when Jesus, the Son of God, walked the earth hundreds of years after Abraham did, He met a man with a crippled arm. In response to this man's need, He didn't say to him, "I see your arm is crippled or is withered" as the King James version puts it. He didn't state what was obvious in the natural. No, He called it the way He saw it. He said to the man, "Stretch out your arm." Why? Because that's the way He saw it … fully functioning and perfectly whole … so that's why He could ask him to do something that in the natural seemed ridiculous. When we begin to see things the way Jesus sees them as already done and begin to call or speak according to what His Word says, we will see them manifested in our lives and situations.

Now, let's turn our attention to the name change that is recorded in the first part of Genesis 17:5. The Lord tells Abram, "Neither shall thy name anymore be called Abram, but thy name shall be called Abraham; for a father of nations have I made thee." As I said earlier, hidden inside this amazing account is a powerful, transformative truth.

I have been a Christian all my life and I was brought up in a Spirit-filled home and church, attended Bible College, heard countless sermons but in all my years of Christian life, I must admit, I didn't truly understand this truth until recently. While studying Genesis 17 over the last couple of years, the Holy Spirit has opened my understanding of this revelation. It has not only impacted my life in a dynamic and awesome way, but also those with whom I have shared this message over the past five years as I have preached this truth.

This book is written to help you as a believer come to a fuller understanding of what The Blessing of Abraham truly is and how this transformative truth can revolutionize your life in a powerful way.

A Very Powerful Revelation!

You see, there's a significant difference between the Hebrew alphabet and the English alphabet and most other languages for that matter. The letters of the English alphabet are just letters with no meaning or significance. Letters make words; words put together convey a thought, and so on. That is not the case in the He-brew language. Every letter of the Hebrew alphabet is a word with a meaning and also has a corresponding pic-ture. For an example of this, if you look at Psalm 119, the longest Psalm in the Bible, in most translations you will see that it is divided into sections and above those sections, are the letters of the Hebrew alphabet … i.e, *aleph*, meaning beginning, first or sacrificial lamb; *bet or beth*, meaning house and so on.

If you travel to Israel as I have many times, as you drive down the highways and roads, you will see street signs such as "Beth-shan" or "Beth-lehem," etc., mean-ing Beth or house of whomever's name follows it. It's where we get the word *Beth-El* or house of God.

When you get to the fifth letter of the Hebrew al-phabet, you come to the letter *He* or *Hey* and sometimes spelled *Hei*. Again, I believe it is significant that it is the fifth letter as five is the number of grace in the Bible. Grace is exactly what the patriarch received and it is captured in the new name given to him by the Lord. To us, it just looks like an "h" was inserted into his name but what was imparted was far greater than just a con-sonant. You see, this letter and word "He" or "Hey" means the Spirit of the Lord. He is the Spirit of Grace, the significance being that apart from the supernatural impartation that Abram received, he would never have received the fulfillment of the promise that he would be the father of many nations or even one son, for that matter. Even more interesting and more revealing is the way that this letter is pronounced! It is not articulated with the lips or the tongue but rather sounds like an exhalation of breath.

When I preach this message, I breathe forcefully into the microphone to further drive home this truth, but I believe you can grasp this awesome truth without the sound effects. Here's the mighty truth contained in this verse. When God inserted the "Hey" or His Spirit into Abram's name and body, He breathed or exhaled His life-giving, healing, restoring, renewing, creative and quickening power into the deadness of Abram's body, making his body like that of a 24-year-old young man who now could father a child. Now, the miracle could take place! Anything that God breathes into comes alive! That is exactly what happened to this 99-year-old man.

The Transforming Power of The Spirit

From that moment on, he was no longer Abram but Abra-ham for the breath of the Spirit was now in him. In that glorious moment, he was translated to a new realm of faith and possibility — an enlarged territory. It's in this place or territory that the miraculous power of the Spirit of the Lord operates.

It is not unlike what happened to Adam in the Garden of Eden. As I said earlier, Adam would have remained a lump of clay if the Lord hadn't breathed into his nostrils, and when He did, Adam became a living soul at that very moment. Romans 8:11 tells us "…if the Spirit of Him who raised Christ from the dead dwell in you, it (He) will quicken [breathe life or make alive, renew, restore, heal] your mortal bodies!" Yes, the very same Holy Spirit that raised Christ from the dead in resurrection power is living and breathing in you and me, bringing us life and that more abundantly. God not only performed this amazing miracle in Abraham's body but also in his wife's body. You will recall that prior to this infilling of the Spirit and impartation of miraculous power, her name was Sarai. When God breathed the *hey* or His Spirit's life giving, restorative breath into her body, He changed her name to Sar-ah. Suddenly, this old woman's womb became like the womb of a 24-year-old woman that could produce an egg, be fertilized and bring to full gestation a perfectly whole male child … not just any child but the son of promise, Isaac.

Let that truth sink into your spiritual consciousness and heart. Whatever He, the Spirit of the Lord, breathes on or into, receives life, health, power, strength, renewal and quickening. Perhaps your health has declined and the doctor's report isn't very encouraging. Perhaps your marriage is strained and the love that was once there seems to have died, and all that's left is going through the motions, or its even further decayed to the point that the word divorce has now been uttered. Worse yet, you feel dead in your spirit and you feel far from the Lord and the intimate fellowship and relationship you once shared with Him now seems a distant memory. Maybe your child, who you raised up in the house of the Lord, wants nothing to do with Him or the things of God.

Don't Give Up!

My friend, if you find yourself experiencing and relating to any of these situations that I have mentioned, or other areas of your life that seem dead, non-productive and hopeless, realize this powerful truth for you today!   There is nothing that you are going through that the breath of the Holy Spirit cannot change and transform! I have experienced it in my life on many occasions and seen situations that once seemed absolutely insurmountable and impossible change, and what was once dead, come back to life. If He did it for me, He can and will do it for you!

Let me remind you, though, it was in the presence of the Almighty, the Lord, God Jehovah-Rapha (the Lord who heals) that quickened and transformed Abraham both spiritually and physically! It is in His presence where we receive power ... resurrection power (Rom. 8:11) ... that heals, delivers, restores, renews and brings back life to the dead areas of our lives.

God honored Abram's step of faith and his ability to believe in God's promise, and that set into motion a wave of favor, miracles and blessings that his descendants are still benefiting from today!

In the chapters that follow, I will give you powerful examples of how this blessing is still operating and is still available to us who live generations after father Abraham. I will share powerful testimonials of its miraculous demonstration in my life and the lives of those I've ministered to and explain also exactly what is included in this blessing as part of our inheritance as the children of Abraham. I encourage you to keep reading because every one of these amazing benefits belongs to you!

CHAPTER TWO

This Is
Your Time!

I can identify and relate to the story of Abram because five and half years ago, I went through an experience in my life and ministry where God literally called me out of all what was familiar and comfortable and thrust me into a new season ... a new expanded land or enlarged territory if you will. I would like to share it with you now to give a current day example and testimony of how the truth I just shared with you in chapter one about the blessing of Abraham has impacted my life and ministry so you know that I am speaking from experience and not just theory. He breathed new direction, new focus and quite literally took my wife and I to a new territory in ministry and ability and since then, I have been amazed at what has occurred in both our personal life as a couple and also in our ministry life. I share it to inspire you to believe for what He has been speaking into your life, your family, your vocation, your business or ministry.

Called To A New Land

For twenty-two years I served faithfully as the Music Minister/Worship Leader and Vice President of Benny Hinn Ministries, traveling the world along side Pastor Benny, a healing evangelist, helping to bring the saving, healing message of the gospel of Jesus Christ to millions around the world. While I counted it a privilege and an honor and enjoyed immensely my work, my colleagues and treasured the moments in God's glory beyond words, yet still something deep down in my heart was longing for and crying out for more. It took me several years to come to fully realize that this unsettledness and restlessness that I was experiencing was not the product of boredom or monotony, or ungratefulness and complacency, but rather the work of the Holy Spirit stirring me and doing a work of enlargement in my heart. He was calling me to "a land that He would show me" and if I was obedient to His call, He would not only guide but provide for me in every way just as He did with faithful Abraham.

Seeds of Blessing

It had begun several years earlier — seven to be exact in January of 2003 — when during a time of fasting and prayer, I read the book *The Prayer of Jabez* by Dr. Bruce Wilkinson. In the book he expounds upon the prayer that Jabez prayed in I Chronicles 4:10, which says, "Oh, that You would bless me indeed, and enlarge my territory, that Your hand would be with me, and that You would keep me from evil, that I may not cause pain!" (NKJV).

Verse 9 of the same chapter distinguishes Jabez as a man of honor for it states that, "Jabez was more honorable than his brothers." We don't know much else about this man and his incredible prayer, for he is not mentioned anywhere else in Scripture. Jabez, who's name means heartache or sorrow, asked the Lord for four things in his prayer.

1. that the Lord would bless him, and not just a little but a lot!
2. that the Lord would enlarge his territory
3. that the Lord's hand would be with him
4. that he would be kept from evil

Although we know very little about Jabez, we do know this: the Lord heard him and granted his request! I believe that if this prayer was important enough to be included in the pages of the Holy Word of God, it is there because He wanted us to not only know about it but to ask Him to do the same in our lives, families, businesses and yes, for those in ministry also with the expectation that God will do the same for us that He did for Jabez.

"You mean it's okay to ask the Lord to bless me?" Absolutely! Scripture tells us "the effectual, fervent prayer of a righteous man avails much" (James 5:16). Jabez wasn't shy in asking the God of Israel to bless him. His fervent prayer produced results. In my opinion, his prayer was also offered in humility as he asked that God's hand would be with him for protection and direction and keep him from evil that he wouldn't cause pain. Remember, 1 Peter 5:6-7 says, "Therefore humble yourselves under the mighty hand of God, that He may exalt you in due time, casting all your care upon Him, for He cares for you" (NKJV).

Jabez is one of many who received the blessing of the Lord based on answered prayer and whose life was forever altered when he prayed similar prophetic prayers. God is not a respecter of persons (Acts 10:34). He will answer your fervent prayer too. "Ask, and it will be given to you; seek, and you will find; knock, and it will be opened to you. For everyone who asks receives, and he who seeks finds, and to him who knocks it will be opened" (Matt. 7:7-8, NKJV).

An Encounter With God at 37,000 Feet

While flying to Mexico in January of 2003, shortly after reading the book, *The Prayer of Jabez* and praying the exact prayer that Jabez did to the Lord, I had an amazing experience at 37,000 feet that I can only describe as awesome … my very own Genesis 17 encounter (as recounted for you in chapter one) if you will. Let me give you a little background about how the experience came about. For a period of time, I also served as the Missions Director for Benny Hinn Ministries as well as Minister of Music, my main area of responsibility. At the time, we were building an orphanage in a city called Tulancingo, which is located about an hour and a half from Mexico City. The task necessitated frequent trips to oversee the project and to work on getting the legal charter, etc. Just prior to the trip, I had been in a time of fasting as was my practice at the beginning of each year and all that I can say is this: shortly after take off, I opened my Bible and began to read the Word of God and pray. For the next 3 hours of the flight, the only way I can describe to you what happened is to say that I was "caught up" spiritually into the Lord's presence and He began to outline my future and the future of my ministry in very specific detail. As I read my Bible, He took me to Joshua 3:7 where God said to Joshua just shortly after Moses' death, "This day will I begin to magnify thee" (KJV).

Those words leaped off the page and as the Holy Spirit was speaking directly to me, I began to think about and wonder, "What does it mean when God begins to magnify you?" Many of us as children played with a magnifying glass and enjoying looking at various bugs, insects, leaves, etc. The magnification of the lens enlarged the most minute details of the object so that you could plainly see things that just seconds ago were hidden from your natural eye. Then it dawned on me that when you magnify an object, you don't change the object you are looking at … that is unless you held the magnifying glass in such a manner that the rays of the sun eventually caused it to begin to burn! What changed was your perspective of the object. Suddenly, you were seeing things you never saw or realized existed before because of the power of magnification.

When the glorious light of God magnifies you, He enlarges your vision to see things that were hidden inside of you that you may not have realized were there all along. Gifts, talents, and abilities that are just waiting for you to discover lay dormant beneath the surface of your spiritual consciousness and now suddenly, in this moment of divine encounter, He is calling them forth into reality to use them to be a blessing to you and to those He has called you to minister to. You see, before others can see your new assignment, your new season, the new territory God has called you to, you must see it for yourself. If you don't see it, you will never experience it! Once Joshua saw that God had truly called him to lead the children of Israel as his mentor Moses had, then Israelites began to recognize him as their leader and responded accordingly.

God was saying to Joshua (Josh. 3:7), "I see in you one that is capable to defeat Israel's enemies and bring My chosen people into the promised land than that I showed your predecessor Moses." Once Joshua saw that, as the result of being magnified by the Lord, He began to wear the authority of that new position like a garment. Something in him rose to the challenge and he developed into exactly the leader that God had seen in him. He had to see it first; once he did, it was only a matter of time and the children of Israel would also!

God spoke to me clearly on that flight to Mexico and showed me that I was not only a Worship/Music minister but that I was called and anointed to preach the Word of God and to be used in the gifts of the Holy Spirit to bring healing, deliverance to God's people and as a Revivalist to the nations. Once I began to see what He had for me, I began to take on the authority of that new position and mantle and in His time, He made it a reality … the reality that I'm living now!

This began a gradual transition into a new season of ministry for me. Although it took seven years to completely come about, for the last five and a half years since January of 2010, I have been seeing the fulfillment of what the Holy Spirit showed me on that flight to Mexico in January of 2003, and it has been so awesome to see it come to pass. Many of the things He showed me about my future on that flight have now come to pass ... some of them just within the last few months. God is faithful to His promises and when He speaks a promise over your life, your ministry, your family, your health, your business or whatever it is — as He did to Abram centuries ago — He will bring it to pass in His perfect timing!

A New Land and A New Place In God

In the example of Abraham, although Abram had nothing in his life or the natural realm that would give any indication that he was about to become a father, once he had that glorious experience in Genesis 17, his faith was quickened to believe (a work of the Spirit of the Lord) and he was elevated to a realm where miracles happen ... a heavenly territory where the supernatural operates ... the place where he now could receive the promise God had given him. God not only took Abram to a physical land or place that he had never been to before but He brought him into a territory in the Spirit, a new level of faith where the impossible is possible.

When God wants to do something extraordinary, supernatural and miraculous in your life, He may need to "take you out, so that He can take you in." Out of what is comfortable, familiar; the abilities, people and sources you have previously trusted in and in to a place where all you can do is trust Him completely to bring about your miracle because you have exhausted all other means, and it can only happen supernaturally. In my case, that is exactly what He did with me. He took me out of the ministry I had been in for 22 years and thrust me into a new season ... with only Him to depend on! That is why I believe He allowed Abram's body to become dead reproductively and Sarai, his wife's womb also, so that when the miracle happened, everyone would know that it had to be the result of divine intervention and the mighty, miracle-working power of God that brought it about.

The prophet Habakkuk also said, "Though the vision tarry [or in other words it will take time to manifest in your life] wait [not a passive state but waiting on the Lord in prayer for His timing] for it" (Hab. 2:3). It took seven years for the vision that the Lord showed me to become reality. Along the way, I asked many times, "When Lord?" He would often confirm it, either through His Word or a circumstance in my life. During those years, I would read and re-read the things that God spoke to my heart and I would speak them out of my mouth as declarations of faith. I believe that not only should we write down the things that God shows us but we should also speak them out of our mouths. Why do you say that? Something happens in the spiritual realm when you speak the Word of the Lord. I believe it activates or sets in motion heavenly and angelic activity to bring about the Word of the Lord. I not only spoke these things out of my mouth in my personal times of prayer and devotion, but I also began to share them with trusted friends who I knew would not only believe me, but would encourage me to believe that they would happen.

Let me give a word of advise here! Surround yourself with people who will celebrate your vision, or what God has shown you and not speak negatively or just tolerate you in a dismissive manner. I was blessed to have my family as well as a few close friends and confidants that I knew I could share my experience with and I am grateful to them for praying it into being with me and not killing my vision with negativity or any inability to recognize what God was doing in me.

Then in January of 2010, seven years to the date almost, I was fasting as is my tradition at the beginning of every year, and in prayer I heard the Lord speak four words to me: "This is your time." They actually came in the form of a chorus or song; here's what He said to my heart and I believe He gave it to me, not just for myself but also for those I minister to. I would like to share it with you. Here are the lyrics He spoke to my heart.

"This is your time for the harvest
This is your year for reward
This is your season of blessing
From the hand of the Lord
The windows of heaven are open
The blessing if outpoured
This is your day, This is your time says the Lord"
— words and music by Jim Cernero

It's Time To Get Out of The Boat!

My spirit leaped in me as I heard those words because I knew it was confirmation that what God had shown me years earlier was about to come to pass. Interestingly, that very day, I visited a local Christian Bookstore and there on the end cap display was Joel Osteen's latest book release, *It's Your Time*. The book title jumped out at me, once again a confirmation that the Holy Spirit was speaking to my heart and He wanted me to confirm that this wasn't just my mind but the Holy Spirit. I picked up a copy of the book and I am so grateful to Joel for writing it because it was such a source encouragement to me as I took what was for me a giant step of faith out of what had been my comfort zone … my boat so to speak, as in the story of Peter from Scripture. When the Lord summoned Peter to step out of the boat and walk on water, He was totally dependent on the Lord to keep him from sinking, and as long as He kept his eyes on the Lord, he achieved the impossible, the miraculous. I have an appreciation for what Peter's thought processes were at that moment because to me, stepping out of what had been my boat of security for 22 years from all that was familiar in every way would have been terrifying, apart from the fact that I had heard the Lord's voice. I knew that as long as I kept my eyes on Him, I would see God operate in the miraculous in my life and ministry, and that is exactly what has happened!

I can't begin to recount for you all the doors that have opened … divine connections that have come my way … and most importantly, the divine enabling, or the anointing that has come as I have opened my mouth to preach and He has filled it as He promised He would do. So you see, that is why I relate to the story of Abraham, our father, and why his testimony has brought a powerful source of encouragement, hope, and faith to my heart and life!

Write The Vision

I don't remember much about the flight details but I do remember that I had a little spiral bound notepad with me and suddenly, under the inspiration of the Spirit of the Lord, I began to "write the vision" as the prophet Habakkuk instructs us to do, and before I knew it, I had filled the entire pad as tears rolled down my cheeks in God's glorious presence. The things that He spoke to me seemed incredible and in my mind I was thinking, how could these things ever come to pass? I couldn't imagine it and yet now, here in 2015 as I write this book, I am living out that very vision, and the very things He showed me on that flight have become reality. I am preaching with ease as if I had been preaching regularly for many years with an authority and unction I know is from the Holy Spirit. I open my mouth and it simply pours out and flows with a continuity that I could never have imagined. I recognize that I am drawing from a deep well that God poured into me of both the knowledge of His Word but also how to operate in the gifts of the Spirit, having been in this arena of the supernatural and classroom of the Holy Spirit for many years! People are getting healed in my services, just as HE showed me; people are being touched by the power of God.

Recently, while preaching in the Dayton, Ohio area, a woman with a broken back was instantaneously healed and all of the excruciating pain she had been in for weeks left her. She tore off her cumbersome back brace that covered her complete torso and walked with hands in the air praising God for relief and the healing that had just happened in God's presence. PTL! An acceleration, if you will, has taken place and things that should have taken much longer to develop have speedily come about. Once again, I don't say this to brag but rather to illustrate for you what can happen when we allow the breath of God's Spirit, the blessing of Abraham, to breathe new life into our visions, dreams, and Godly plans.

I don't believe God gave me this revelation nor has had me experience it in my life just for me. I believe that He wants me to share it with you to encourage you to begin to believe Him for supernatural things to happen just like they did for Abraham and his wife Sarah, and to countless others in the Word of God and more recently, in my life. In fact, that's why I have written this book! To help you believe that if God could do it for me, He certainly can do it for you! God's plans and purposes are different for all of us, but His Word is the same to all!

Perhaps you have heard Him speak enlargement over you and at one point you were full of anticipation for an answer to that prayer of your heart, that dream or desire … that hope for that job promotion or that blessing financially or maybe an expanded ability in ministry … but now that the years have gone by, it's just a fading, distant memory. Let me speak life into your vision and encourage you that just as He did with Abraham, just as He did in my life, He does NOT forget His Word, nor His promises and He will bring them to pass in His perfect time. In fact, I believe "this is your time" for the blessing!

You may be asking yourself, "How can you say that, Jim?" That's a good question! I happen to believe the Word of God, that's why! I believe that the Bible is the inspired revelation of God's heart for you and me, and if we will take the time to read it and ask God's Spirit to help us understand it and bring revelation to our hearts and minds, He will do just that.

What's In A Name?

For example, there is significance in even the names of some of the great prophets and patriarchs contained in the Word of God. In those days, when the Word of God was being given by divine inspiration to the prophets, their names were indicative of their character, their destiny, or who they were as a person or figure in relation to Israel, God's chosen people.

I have always been encouraged by one of the prophets in the Old Testament by the name of Zechariah. Here's why! The familiar words of the verse found in Zechariah 4:6 that most of us in the church can recite with ease declares, "Not by might, nor by power, but by My Spirit, says the Lord of Hosts." We know the words but many believers don't know that these words were spoken by the prophet Zechariah to a man by the name of Zerubbabel, whose job it was to repair the walls of the city of Jerusalem when they returned from a long captivity in the ancient country of Babylon which today is just south of present day Iraq.

God Remembers

The prophet Zechariah's name means "God re-members"! God is not like man who sometimes for-gets his/her promise or goes back on one's word! When God says it, you can count on the fact that it will come to pass! So, when you're tempted to think that God has forgotten about you, your situation or your prob-lem, let the fact that He used a man/prophet with the name Zechariah in part just to remind you that He re-members! When I preach this, I have the congregation speak that phrase out; why don't you do that right now! Say, "God Remembers!" I promise you, something will begin to take root in you and faith will begin to grow once again.

God Blesses

Would you like to know what Zechariah's father's name was? I assure you, you will be blessed once I tell you! Zechariah's father's name was Berechiah and his name means "God blesses"! It's God's nature and de-sire to bless His children! All through the Word of God there are passages of scripture telling us of this fact. Not only does He desire to bless us, but His blessing is on every aspect of our lives: in our health, our finances, our spirit, our marriage and our vocations. Like you spoke out of your mouth what Zechariah's name means, "God remembers!" now do the same the meaning of his father Berechiah's name. Declare it! "God Blesses!"

At The Appointed Time

Amazingly, His grandfather's name was also VERY significant and I pray that knowing what it means brings you encouragement, hope and faith to believe God wants to bless you ... now! Zechariah's Grandfather's name was Iddo, which means "at the appointed time!" God will remember, God will bless and He will do it ... at the appointed time. In other words, God knows exactly when to fulfill His promises to us and when to carry out His Word in our lives. His timing is always perfect and if we will trust Him, He will see to it that "all things work together for good" (Rom. 8:28).

As one last confession, speak the meaning of Zechariah's grandfather Iddo's name out in faith: Say (it) to your Spirit, your inner man. Say, "This is my appointed time." My God will remember! He will bless and He will do it "at the appointed time!" I believe your faith is increasing as you have made these prophetic declarations out of your mouth and very soon, dreams, visions, answers to prayer, breakthroughs, miracles and supernatural things will happen as a result of it! Amen!

I believe that part of His mandate to me is to declare this message to those who hear me preach and those who read my writings: "This is your time!" It is time to believe and receive from Him the blessing that He has for you! It is time for your wilderness or dry season to end and time to come into the abundance He has just waiting for you. It is time for your prayers to be answered! It is time for your season of lack to come to an end! This is your time!

CHAPTER THREE

The Blessing of Grace

The letter/word "hey" which I defined for you in chapter one, was the Hebrew letter that God inserted into Abram's name, making him Abraham, also means "the Spirit of Grace." Grace is the conduit through which all blessing from the Lord comes to us. Apart from the grace of God, we could never experience all that the Lord purchased for us on Calvary. It is by grace that all the blessings that Christ purchased for us with His blood come to us. Only His infinite and amazing grace qualifies us to receive that favor from God and is simply to be received, not earned or worked for. When God breathes on your life, along with that divine breath comes supernatural favor and blessing. Throughout the Bible, the number 5 is referred to as the number of Grace. One of the strongest proofs of this is the fact that as I mentioned earlier, this word *hey* is the fifth letter of the Hebrew alphabet but there are many more examples throughout the Word of God.

Grace and Mercy

We often use the words grace and mercy interchangeably but actually they are somewhat different in meaning. I like how Joseph Prince puts it: Mercy means we DON'T get what we DO deserve! What don't we get as a result of the mercy of the Lord? We don't get: condemnation, shame, judgment, punishment, failure, loss, poverty and even death. However, grace means just the reverse. What DO we get that we DON'T deserve as a result of God's infinite grace towards us? Instead of punishment, judgment , shame and even death as I mention above, because of God's amazing love for us, and through His grace, we get what we don't deserve such as: forgiveness, no condemnation, protection, favor, righteousness, peace, and the blessing a hope and a future eternally with Christ Jesus. It is by grace that all the blessings that Christ purchased for us with His blood come to us. Today we are grateful for both His abundant mercy and grace coming to us all by the blessing of the Spirit of Grace living and breathing in us!

His Grace and The Miraculous

The story recorded for us in Zechariah chapter four brings further revelation to the fact that when the Spirit of Grace breathes in your direction, miraculous things can and will happen. You will recall that the prophet Zechariah spoke this mighty Word of the Lord to a man by the name of Zerubbabel. Zerubbabel was in charge of rebuilding the city of Jerusalem after their long captivity in Babylon. As happens to all of us at times, Zerubbabel became discouraged because he was receiving opposition from the surrounding countries and it was preventing him from accomplishing the work of the Lord. The enemy of our souls hates the work of God and hates the man or woman of God who tries to accomplish it. He will do everything he can to bring discouragement, confusion and try to prevent it from being successful. That is why we have to stay focused on the Word of the Lord which gives us the strength to carry on and persist, no matter what obstacle may be standing in our way!

So God sent a prophet to Zerubbabel by the name of Zechariah to encourage him. God always has the right Word for us in our time of need! Zechariah, under the inspiration of the Spirit of the Lord, speaks these famous words to him: "not by might, nor by power but by my Spirit says the Lord of Hosts" (Zech. 4:6). He was telling Zerubbabel to stop trying to make it happen in his own strength, ability, intellect and even financial means, and let God do it. He was saying, I can accomplish in one divine moment what cannot be made to happen in hours, days, weeks, months, and even years in the natural. He tells him to prophesy TO the mountain and challenge its authority. "Who are you mountain standing in the way of Zerubbabel?" Sometimes you not only have to speak to God about the mountain or Goliath (giant) standing in your way! You have to speak to THE MOUNTAIN or GOLIATH and say, "Who do you think you are standing in the way of Lord?" When God's Spirit of grace comes upon you like it did Zerubbabel, it will cause miraculous things to happen!

In the next verse — verse 7 — we discover what would prophetically be the outcome when he (Zerubbabel) obeyed the word of the Lord and spoke to the mountain. "Thou shalt become a plain: [the problem that was likened to a mountain standing before him and blocking his success or achievement] and he shall bring forth the headstone thereof with shoutings, crying, Grace, grace unto it." The prophet Zechariah assured Zerubbabel that when he did what the Spirit of the Lord was telling him to do, the result would be a divine and supernatural intervention by God in the situation, and God would cause him to be successful in completing the task he was called to do to bring about a victory. Notice it says, "He shall bring forth the headstone." The headstone was the very last stone to be put in place when construction of an edifice or wall was being built. The placement of the headstone represented symbolically that the work was done … that it had been accomplished. That is why Jesus cried, "It is finished!" because the Bible tells in Ephesians 2:20 that He was the chief Cornerstone or headstone. In other words, when He cried, "It is finished" or "tetelesti" in the original Greek language of the New Testament, He was saying I have finished the work of salvation and accomplished the Will of the Father forever. We can cease from our labors and rest in the finished work of the Lord on Calvary knowing He already took care of whatever it is we are struggling with. He has already provided the grace and power to provide all our need and for every hindering spirit to be defeated. All we need to do is speak "grace, grace unto it" and watch the Spirit of the Lord bring it about!

A Special Word To Pastors

Very often when I minister in a church for the first time, the Holy Spirit will impress on me to call the pastor and his wife … sometimes the entire pastoral team … to come forward. I will then ask the congregation to stretch their hands out towards them and prophetically speak out of their mouths to them "grace, grace to it." You might ask why do that? The same demons that challenged Zerubbabel's work, the work of the Lord in rebuilding the walls of Jerusalem, are still fighting and opposing the work of the Lord today. Pastors (and their families) are prime targets for their attacks and sadly today, we hear instance after instance of pastors leaving the ministry, closing down what were once great churches and giving up because they are quite frankly tired of the fight. This should not be, church! This should not happen when God has given us His Spirit of Grace like He did to Zerubbabel and His power to fulfill His divine plan! Instead of gossiping and perhaps tearing down the pastors, we the body of Christ need to be speaking "grace, grace to it!" and believe that the same Holy Spirit that came on Zerubbabel when He heard the Word of the Lord by the prophet Zechariah, "not by might, nor by power but by My Spirit says the Lord of Hosts" (Zech 4:6) will breathe on our pastors, renewing them, giving them courage and faith to believe and hope, which is the confidant expectation of good. I can't tell you how many of the pastors and wives that I have done this for have said afterwards, "I feel fresh fire, fresh vision and new life to do the work that the Lord has called me to do!" Let this story and these powerful words be an encouragement to you right now as I speak them over your life through the pages of this book under the anointing of the Holy Spirit. "Grace to it! Man or woman of God, the breath of the Holy Spirit breathe in you right now and quicken you, empower you with His divine grace, ability and power to accomplish what He has called you do in the Name of Jesus!"

I not only do this for the pastors and staff, but I will often have the members of the congregation think of that need, that obstacle to their faith, that physical or emotional problem, that relationship issue, that financial bondage and tell them to place their hands on their heart and to speak "grace, grace to it!" As they speak these words, I encourage them to believe that the same Spirit of the Lord that breathed into Father Abraham, is breathing His abundant grace into them, their situations, their needs and will bring about the victory for them in the Name of the Lord of Hosts, the Name of Jesus! Praise God! Many have received their healing right then and there as a result of this exercise in faith.

I recently preached in a great church in Mobile, Alabama. In the course of my message, under the anointing of the Holy Spirit I felt impressed to have the people place their hand on their body if they were suffering from a physical ailment or to think of the problem or situation that was causing them distress and standing in the way of their victory and say, "Grace, grace to it!" After the service, a woman came up to the pastor and testified that the moment she spoke the words, her back was instantly healed! Praise the Lord!

By the way, while I was preaching and ministering in that same service, I had Greg Wiggins, who was the worship leader for the church, and is currently the keyboardist/musical director for Pastor Benny Hinn (he and I are part of a unique club of two people who have ever held that position) play softly behind me. My ministry flow is very much affected by music, having that as a dual aspect of my ministry and so often, if the keyboardist in the church I'm ministering at is accomplished and anointed, I will ask them to continue playing softly as I begin to preach and some times throughout the whole time I'm preaching and ministering. Greg had been playing the whole time I preached and continued to play as I was ministering in Words of Knowledge about people who were being healed. Several had been healed and I was just about to turn the service back to Pastor Joel Grantham, the pastor, when the Spirit led me to say, "Someone here has a terrible sinus problem and the Lord wants to heal it." Little did I know that throughout the entire service, Greg had been suffering with his sinuses and was miserable, needing a touch from the Lord. As soon as I called the Word of Knowledge out about someone being healed in their sinuses, Greg spoke up and said, "It's me!" I immediately asked him to leave the keyboard and come up to be prayed for. When we laid hands on him, he was immediately healed! Praise the Lord!

God Is Faithful

I mention this particular healing here because I feel it's important for those who minister to others regularly to realize this: while you are faithfully ministering to others, the Holy Spirit won't forget about your need! If necessary, He will give a Word to someone who is ministering or in whatever way is necessary to bring about your healing or provide the answer to your need. Many times throughout the years of travel and ministry I have wondered would I have the strength to make it through the many services and hours of ministry that were ahead of me, but God has poured out His immeasurable grace just when I needed it and enabled me to minister in His Name.

Removing The Roadblocks

What are you facing today? What is standing in your way of divine health? What situation has come against your finances or your family life or your business or your marriage? I challenge you to pray in the Spirit and then do as the prophet Zechariah instructed Zerubbabel to do; speak "Grace, grace to it" and watch God intervene and bring about your miracle. In fact, let me pray this over you right here, right now. Note though, Zerubbabel's prayer was "after" the Spirit of the Lord came on him which made his prayer more than just words spoken out of his mouth, but elevated it to the prophetic or supernatural realm. Spend some time in God's Holy presence through worship and prayer, letting Him breathe on your heart and into your spirit His quickening prayer and then pray this prayer and watch God's Spirit bring it about as you speak "grace, grace to it!"

"Father, we know that every Word of Scripture is God-breathed and recorded for our benefit so right now we speak "grace, grace to it" to whatever has become an obstacle in the way of my dear friend who is reading this book. Grace to their bodies and healing in the Name of Jesus. Grace to their marriage which seems like it is at an impasse and that there's no hope of being healed. Grace to their finances and that bank account that seems never to have enough. Grace to that child that is away from the Lord or getting involved in drugs or in rebellion, to bring about divine reconciliation and restoration of faith. Grace! Grace to it! Be healed, delivered, breathed on by the Spirit of the Lord. We thank you for mighty victories in Jesus' Name, Amen!"

A Note To The Reader

If you prayed that prayer with me and have spoken "grace, grace to it," now believe God and expect Him to supernaturally intervene and bring about your answer! I encourage you to write to me at the email address I have included here and tell me of how God supernaturally intervened as a result of this prophetic prayer. info@certainsoundministries.org

His very essence or nature is grace. HE, the Holy Spirit, is the Divine Executor of the Father's Will, recorded for us in the Word and paid for by the blood of Jesus, the Son of God. I like to say it this way: the Word of God is "the Living Will" of the Father, paid for by the Son and made available to us through the Spirit ... the Spirit of Grace. The Heavenly contract was signed by the precious blood of Jesus when He died for us on the cross. Not reading the Word of God or studying the scripture to discover all that is ours in Christ is like the children of a rich man not bothering to attend the reading of his will and thereby never knowing and forfeiting what his or her father's intention was for them. As a

Last Will and Testament of an earthly man or woman in a sense speaks from the grave their wishes for their loved ones, so the blood of Jesus speaks to us eternally of the will of God for us, His children, and our divine inheritance as believers and children of the Most High (Heb. 12:24).

A Glimpse of Grace

When thinking about the subject of grace and where it is depicted in the Bible, the beautiful story of Ruth and the favor she experienced is, in my opinion, a perfect picture of the grace of the Lord. Just as He orchestrated the steps of Ruth's life, so God will position us for divine favor and redeem our lives from what may seemingly be devastating or dead end circumstances if we allow His Holy Spirit to do so!

Ruth was from the country of Moab and was the daughter-in-law of Naomi, who was an Israelite from the city of Bethlehem. Naomi's husband, Elimelech, had moved the family from Bethlehem during a drought to Moab to provide for his family. After several years there, Naomi's husband died, and eventually her two sons, Mahlon and Chilion, married Moabite women: Orphah and Ruth. Sadly, Naomi's two sons also died about ten years later, leaving their wives, Ruth and Orphah, as widows along with their mother-in-law, Naomi.

After their deaths, Naomi heard that the Lord had restored the land of her birth, Israel, with food and abundance so she decided to return home. She told her two daughters-in-law to go back to their families, blessed them and said good-bye. Orphah decided to return to her people, but Ruth pledged to stay with her mother-in-law, Naomi, and the two of them returned to Israel. The divine decision that Ruth made set in motion a literal and spiritual harvest in not only her life but in the generations to follow, including you and me!

Upon returning to Israel, they found themselves in a destitute position without food or provision of any kind. Little did they know that God was about to shower them with His grace and favor and completely turn their lives around, restoring back to them more than what they had lost.

The Right Place, The Right Time

Location, location, location … this is a phrase we hear often with regard to whether a business will be successful or a property will increase in value. It's also true in the spiritual realm. Our harvest … our season of increase … is often connected to our location … not just our geographical location but our location in proximity to the heart of God. Ruth 1:22 says, speaking of Naomi, Ruth's mother-in-law, "and they came to Bethlehem in the beginning of barley harvest." The decision to move to back to Bethlehem triggered a harvest on Naomi, Ruth, and her entire family.

A Word To YOU

What is the Lord saying to you? Where is He telling you that you need to go or stay? Where do you belong? Perhaps He's drawing you into closer fellowship with His Spirit. Be sensitive to His voice and listen carefully for this might just be the beginning of your recovery and season of increase.

It so "happened" that Naomi had a kinsman of her husband, Elimelech, who was a man of great wealth; his name was Boaz. Boaz in scripture is a type or foreshadow of Jesus, our Kinsman-Redeemer who has shown us His grace (favor) and desires to bless us. You will see this clearly as I continue to describe for you the events that happened next in this amazing story of grace and favor! Ruth said to Naomi in Ruth 2:2: "Let me go to the fields and pick up the leftover grain behind anyone in whose eyes I find favor" (NIV). The King James version uses the word grace in place of the word favor.

Now watch this, Ruth didn't realize it, but of all the fields that she could have chosen to go and glean corn, she "happens" to pick the one belonging to Boaz, the kinsman of Naomi. By divine providence, she was led to that field to be positioned for favor. As the story goes, Boaz, who again, is a type of Christ in the Bible, a picture of our kinsmen, in that Jesus came to earth in the form of a human baby like us, takes note of Ruth and decides to show her favor.

Faithfulness and Favor

Have you ever felt unappreciated or that your loyalty has been overlooked? Ruth could have felt that way, but as it turned out, someone was taking note of it all along and rewarded her with great favor. Ruth 2:11 says, "Boaz [a type of Christ] replied, I've been told all about what you have done for your mother-in-law since the death of your husband…" In verse 12 Boaz continues to speak, saying, "The Lord repay your work, and a full reward be given you by the Lord God of Israel, under whose wings you have come for refuge." Ruth's faithfulness and loyalty triggered a harvest of favor from Boaz which became the salvation of her entire family. Even though you may feel overlooked, remember the Lord is watching! He will reward your faithfulness with great favor!

He instructs his workers to let "handfuls of purpose" fall deliberately so that Ruth can glean them and have enough food to take home for her and Naomi. In fact, he tells her not to go anywhere else to glean but his field, and he warns his young single workers to not even get any idea about making advances toward her!

Ruth is amazed at the favor she has been shown by this man Boaz, and goes home to tell Naomi about it, bringing the sheaves of grain he has so graciously allowed her to glean. After inquiring about where Ruth had gleaned, Naomi realizes that this man is the kinsmen of her late husband and that the Lord God of Israel is surely in this.

A word about the culture in that day is helpful here. When a man died without children or heirs, it was necessary that a family member not only purchase or redeem the property that formerly belonged to the deceased man and his wife, but also to marry her to carry on the name of the deceased. In this case, Naomi's husband, Elimelech, was deceased as well as his sons, one of which Ruth had been married to. The word would go about the situation and the next in line by relation was to step up and honor the dead in the above described manner. If the next in line was not able to marry the widow, then it would proceed until an appropriate husband was found.

God's Plan Revealed

Naomi being well aware of this culture, instructed Ruth to go back in the evening after the day's work is done and after Boaz has had his evening meal and has laid down to rest. She told her to lift up his skirt (in those days men wore long garments that went down to their feet) and lay there until morning. There's a powerful symbolism in this gesture! It is a perfect picture of Christ, our Kinsmen-Redeemer, covering us with His precious blood when we lay down our lives at His feet.

When Boaz awoke and discovered her there, lying at his feet, he knew that she was a virtuous woman and in keeping with the cultural mandate I mentioned earlier, he went to the gate of the city (where all business transaction took place in those days) to inquire if there was a legitimate next of kin to marry Ruth. He meets the man that is next in line as a kinsmen there at the gate and explains the situation. However, this man was not able to marry Ruth so this cleared Boaz to do so.

Boaz takes Ruth as his wife and soon she bares him a son. Do you see the picture of Christ, purchasing us, the church, His bride, and making us part of his family here? Naomi, Ruth's mother-in-law, becomes the nurse for the child and in her old age, is restored to her family once again. In fact, the women of the village said, "Blessed be the Lord, which has not left you this day without a kinsmen…" (Ruth 4:14). "And may he [prophetically speaking of Christ] be to you a restorer of life and a nourisher of your old age; for your daughter-in-law, who loves you, who is better to you than seven sons, has borne him" (Ruth 4:15).

Restoration and Redemption

The presence of Christ by His Holy Spirit in your life causes Him to be the restorer of life! When God's blessing of grace and favor are breathed into your life, He redeems the past, its mistakes and failures, its shattered pieces and broken dreams, and restores your life back to the abundant life that God originally intended for you and me. I believe that He will also not only give you more years or extend your life but will also cause those years to be quality years, for the Word says of Him, "Who satisfies your mouth with good things, So that your youth is renewed like the eagle's" (Ps. 103: 5). An eagle's beak and feathers continually replenish themselves throughout the course of its life time which would be why the scripture makes reference to their youth being renewed.

Remember, the Holy Spirit, who lives within us when we accept Christ as our Savior, our Kinsmen-Redeemer, is the Spirit of Grace. His presence in your life will cause them to say of you what they said of Naomi: "Blessed be the Lord, which has not left you this day without a kinsmen ... and they will know that He is "the restorer of life and a nourisher in your old age" (Ruth 4:14-15).

Ruth found her deliverance, her life restoration, incredible grace and favor in the presence of her Kinsman-Redeemer, Boaz. Boaz in scripture is a type or shadow of our Lord Jesus Christ, our Kinsman-Redeemer. It is in His presence that grace flows into our lives the same way it did into this amazing woman, Ruth.

There's an amazing verse in Habakkuk 3:4 that underscores this powerful truth. "His radiance [or His person and presence] is like the sunlight; He has rays flashing from His hand, and *there* is *the hiding of His power*." (NAS) Notice, God's power is hidden in His presence! His radiance is the reflected glory of God, His presence. When your spirit feels the warmth of His radiant or Shekinah glory, you are divinely connected to a heavenly source of power ... resurrection power. The result is an outpouring of grace ... grace for miracles, grace for deliverance, grace for reconciliation, grace for provision and so much more! This is all yours and mine as part of the Blessing of Abraham. His abundant grace brings to us all of the aspects of the blessing that I will detail for you as you keep reading.

CHAPTER FOUR

The Blessing of Salvation and Righteousness

Salvation, in my opinion, is one of the greatest blessings extended to you and me. Acts 16:31 says, "So they said, 'Believe on the Lord Jesus Christ, and you will be saved, you and your household.'" Romans 10:9 says, "If you confess with your mouth the Lord Jesus and believe in your heart that God has raised Him from the dead, you will be saved" (NKJV).

The act of getting saved or coming to salvation is really quite simple. According to Romans 10:9 as stated above, it comes down to believing and confessing! Aren't you glad that God didn't complicate things the way some men do when it came to restoring us back to relationship and fellowship that was lost when Adam and Eve sinned in the garden? At times man's approach involves works in order to become worthy, but there is nothing we can do in our own strength to be worthy of this free gift of salvation. The plan of salvation is quite easy to understand and receive. Just believe on the Lord with your heart, confess Him as your Savior with your mouth, and you are saved. Simple ... yet profound and transformative ... and the transformation takes place in a moment, yet it affects us today, tomorrow, and for eternity!

Believe!

It doesn't get any clearer than that! Believing on the Lord is the essential element for redemption (to be bought back from the wicked one), and it transfers the righteousness of Christ to us through the work of the Holy Spirit. The connection between believing and righteousness goes all the way back to Father Abraham. Just as our Father Abraham's right believing transferred righteousness to him, so as part of our inheritance, it is transferred to us. "Abraham believed God and it was accounted to him for righteousness" (Gal. 3:6). This has always been God's way of reconciliation, redemption and righteousness. Abraham simply believed God and that transferred to him righteousness.

One of the most glorious benefits of the Blessing of Abraham is the fact that just as Abraham's faith in God was attributed to him for righteousness, so when we believe on the Lord Jesus Christ as our Savior, we receive the inheritance of righteousness. This comes to us, not because of any works that we have done, but simply because of His mercy. This is stated in Scripture: "Not by works of righteousness which we have done, but according to his mercy he saved us, by the washing of regeneration, and renewing of the Holy Ghost" (Titus 3:5). This is the very same Spirit that Abraham encountered and that breathed life into his and Sarah's bodies!

What a joy it has been for me to see multiplied thousands come to the saving knowledge of the Lord Jesus in massive crusades around the US and internationally! All we need to do is present Him to those who don't know Him and ask the Holy Spirit to do the rest! As we approach the time of Christ's return to earth, we must take every opportunity to share the love of Christ, His power to save, transform and deliver from sin, bondage, and addiction and ask God's Spirit to water the seed we sow for a harvest of souls for the Kingdom of Christ.

As we watch the nightly news and read on the internet how an increasing number of Christians around the world are being persecuted by a false religion and a false God, and many martyred for their faith, it becomes very clear that the church of Jesus Christ — those who are called by His Name — needs to rise up in the power of the Spirit and proclaim the gospel: the good news of salvation through Jesus Christ! It is the same gospel that the Lord preached to Abraham (Gal. 3:8) "And the scripture, foreseeing that God would justify the heathen through faith, preached before the gospel [before Jesus came to earth and preached and lived out the gospel] unto Abraham, saying, in you shall all the nations be blessed [breathed on by the Spirit of God and come to know Jesus, the Messiah, the Savior of the world by the power of the Holy Spirit]."

It is my determination and passion, with the years I have left on this planet to spread the gospel with the help and power of the Holy Spirit to the nations. I pray it is yours also!

This blessing of salvation opens the door to many other blessings that affect every aspect of our lives from that moment on.

The Blessing of Righteousness

Righteousness can never be earned or merited by our actions! It is the result of right believing! Righteousness is imputed or transferred to us by the Holy Spirit as He is the doer in the Godhead and carries out the Will of the Father and the Work of our Lord, Jesus Christ which He paid for with His blood on Calvary for us. As part of our inheritance as the children of Abraham, we too receive the blessing of righteousness or right standing with God. When God looks at us, He doesn't see our sin, our past, our failures or impurity; He sees the blood of His Son and that blood says, "Not guilty!" He sees the spotless perfection of the precious Lamb of God who has forever washed away our sin and made us righteous!

We see this divinely foreshadowed for us in the Old Testament in the sacrifices that the priests made on behalf of Israel's sins. Leviticus 9:2 says, "And he said unto Aaron, Take thee a young calf for a sin offering and a ram for a burnt offering, without blemish, and offer them before the Lord." I want to draw your attention to the fact God instructed Moses to tell Aaron, his brother and who was the priest, to offer two different offerings to the Lord: a calf for a sin offering and a ram for a burnt offering.

The Sin Offering

With the sin offering a spotless animal was laid on the altar and just before killing the animal, which was a picture of our Lord who would one day become the perfect, sacrificial spotless Lamb of God, the priest would lay hands on the animal and in so doing, he was transferring all of the guilt, sin, and shame of all Israel onto the animal. This is a perfect picture of the work of the Lord who was "slain from the foundations of the world." Just as the sins of Israel were transferred to the spotless, pure animal, so our sins and iniquities, our filth and shame were transferred to the Lord when He became our Holy Sacrifice. Praise His glorious name forever!

Once this sin offering had been offered, when God looked down upon Israel, for an entire year, He no longer saw their rebellion, their sin or their shame; He saw the blood which was a token or a sign of righteousness and Israel was counted righteous. So when God looks down at you and me, if He sees the blood of His crucified Son on our hearts, He sees us as righteous and forgiven, not sinful and worthy of punishment because His Son already took the punishment for us and paid our debt. But it doesn't stop there, thankfully! There was also the burnt offering as the scripture from Leviticus mentioned.

The Burnt Offering

After the sin offering, the priest would also offer a burnt offering to the Lord, which involved the sacrifice of another spotless, pure animal. After placing the second animal on the altar, the priest would lay his hands on the animal before slaying it. In this providential act, the opposite of what took place with the sin of-fering happened. When this sacrifice was offered, the purity and spotless, blameless nature of the animal was transferred back to Israel. Hallelujah! Remember that when the priest laid hands on the sin offering, the sins of Israel were transferred to the spotless animal. Now with the burnt offering, the purity, and spotless nature of the Lamb, was transferred back to Israel. God not only wanted their sin to be covered but He also want-ed to impute His righteousness back to them, and that is exactly what transpired when the priest offered the burnt offering.

Now, when God looked down on Israel, He saw them spotless and sinless because the blood made an atonement (purchased their pardon) and covered them. So, when God looks down at us, He sees the covering of His Son's precious blood and sees us cleansed: forgiven, Holy and righteous because of our burnt offering, His Son, Jesus.

Today, as part of the blessing of Abraham, Jesus has become both our sin offering and our burnt offering! Not only were our sins and iniquities transferred to Him on the cross, but His righteousness, His purity and per-fection was transferred to us in the heavenly process! Praise God! That is why we can stand on and claim 2 Corinthians 5:21 which says, "For He has made Him to be sin for us, who knew no sin, that we might be made the righteousness of God in Him."

I have preached a powerful message entitled "The Blood Says So" based on the scripture found in He-brews 12:24 which says, "And to Jesus the mediator of the new covenant, and to the blood of sprinkling, that speaks better things than that of Abel." I won't go into detail on all of the truth and revelation that is contained in this passage except to say that one thing is clear: the blood of Jesus speaks wonderful things over our lives as believers. Just as a Last Will and Testament, in effect, speaks the wishes of the deceased person from the grave so to speak as far as the allocation and distribution of his/her estate, so the blood of Jesus speaks the Will of the Father for us, His inheritance, and the Holy Spirit is the One who executes or carries out that will, distributing the divine blessings to those who are in Christ Jesus.

In my message I go into many of the powerful things that the blood speaks, the first being it speaks redemption and righteousness to us. It speaks redemption in Isaiah 53:5, which says, "He was wounded for our transgressions [our acts of sin], bruised [the original is more closely crushed] for our iniquities [generational curses and sins of the fathers]; the chastisement [punishment] of our peace [the word shalom in Hebrew which means total well-being; body, soul, spirit, mind and everything that touches our lives including our finances] was upon Him and with His stripes we are healed." Jesus' blood speaks redemption to every part of us, and it is our part to agree with what it is says and apply that redemptive blood to our lives and households. Amen!

Abraham was asked by God to do something that no other man had been asked to do ... to offer his only, beloved son of promise as a sacrifice on Mt. Moriah. In the natural, who in their right mind would ever consider doing such a thing ... especially after being childless for nearly 100 years? Yet, Abraham responded obediently to God and made his way up Mt. Moriah with Isaac, trusting God with each step he took.

Perhaps you are familiar with this well-known story recorded in Genesis chapter 22 of Abraham and Isaac. However, it is much more than a man's obedience and surrender to God. This account also presents a divine picture of the perfect work of Jesus Christ our Lord, Who became the spotless Lamb of God for us on the Cross.

Genesis 22:1-13 (NKJ) declares: "Now it came to pass after these things that God tested Abraham, and said to him, 'Abraham!' And he said, 'Here I am.' 2 Then He said, "Take now your son, your only son Isaac, whom you love, and go to the land of Moriah, and offer him there as a burnt offering on one of the mountains of which I shall tell you."

3 So Abraham rose early in the morning and saddled his donkey, and took two of his young men with him, and Isaac his son; and he split the wood for the burnt offering, and arose and went to the place of which God had told him. 4 Then on the third day Abraham lifted his eyes and saw the place afar off. 5 And Abraham said to his young men, "Stay here with the donkey; the lad and I will go yonder and worship, and we will come back to you."

6 So Abraham took the wood of the burnt offering and laid it on Isaac his son; and he took the fire in his hand, and a knife, and the two of them went together. 7 But Isaac spoke to Abraham his father and said,

"My father!" And he said, "Here I am, my son." Then he said, "Look, the fire and the wood, but where is the lamb for a burnt offering?"

8 And Abraham said, "My son, God will provide for Himself the lamb for a burnt offering." So the two of them went together. 9 Then they came to the place of which God had told him. And Abraham built an altar there and placed the wood in order; and he bound Isaac his son and laid him on the altar, upon the wood. 10 And Abraham stretched out his hand and took the knife to slay his son.

11 But the Angel of the Lord called to him from heaven and said, "Abraham, Abraham!" So he said, "Here I am." 12 And He said, "Do not lay your hand on the lad, or do anything to him; for now I know that you fear God, since you have not withheld your son, your only son, from Me."

13 Then Abraham lifted his eyes and looked, and there behind him was a ram caught in a thicket by its horns. So Abraham went and took the ram, and offered it up for a burnt offering instead of his son. 14 And Abraham called the name of the place, The-Lord-Will-Provide;[b] as it is said to this day, "In the Mount of the Lord it shall be provided."

God's Redemptive Plan of Salvation

Do you see it? Do you see the plan of salvation and redemption, the work of righteousness being transferred in this amazing story in Genesis? Abraham represents the Father ... Father God who "so loved the world that He gave His only begotten Son that whoever believes on

Him might be saved" (John 3:16). Isaac, Abraham's beloved son, represents Jesus, the only begotten Son of the Father and beloved of His Father, who willingly came to earth, carried the cross just as Isaac carried the wood in obedience to his father, Abraham, up to Mt. Moriah.

Just as Abraham was about to obey God and put the knife to his beloved son, Isaac, and kill him, he heard an Angel of the Lord call his name, saying, "Abraham, Abraham" and he replied, "Here I am." The Angel of the Lord continued saying, "Don't lay your hand on him; for now I know that you fear God, since you have not withheld your only son from Me."

Imagine the intensity of the moment for both Abraham and his son, Isaac, in those moments as God intervened in the situation and provided a sacrifice! What a flush of relief must have swept over them both as Abraham looked up and saw a ram caught in the thicket (not to mention Isaac!) The thicket represents the crown of thorns that was cruelly placed on the head of Jesus, the precious Lamb of Glory, and the ram also represents Jesus, our sacrifice who took our place on Calvary just as the ram took Isaac's place on Mt. Moriah. What a perfect picture of the eternal plan of salvation ... the blessing of redemption and righteousness which is ours as the children of Abraham.

Before we go on, I want to ask you if you have received the free gift of salvation? Have you confessed with your mouth the Lord Jesus Christ and believed in your heart that God raised Him from the dead? If you have not, there is no better time than right now to pause and pray this prayer:

Prayer:

"Lord Jesus, I acknowledge that you are the Christ, the Son of God, and I believe that You died on the cross for my sins so that I can be saved. I believe that You rose from the dead as the Bible says. Please forgive me of my sin and cleanse my heart. Grant me the greatest gift of salvation today. Be the Savior and Lord of my life today. Amen."

If you prayed this prayer, the blessing of Abraham, including the blessings of salvation and righteousness, are yours. Whatever you need, God has the answer. He loves you and will bestow all the blessings He promised to Abraham upon your life. Receive them by faith and enjoy the new life in Christ that you have begun today!

Just another thought on this aspect of the Blessing of Abraham. I know that currently the phrase "greasy grace" has been thrown around referring to certain preachers who put a strong emphasis on grace and even go as far as to say we never need to repent or ask forgiveness. For the record, I am not among them.

However, I do believe that when the Spirit of the Lord, who is the Spirit of Grace comes to your life, He not only convicts us of sin, but He convicts us of the fact that Jesus completed the work for our salvation and righteousness on the cross! We need to ask for a greater revelation of His grace and what it has provided for us. Nothing can be added because He cried "It is finished!" No amount of striving against sin or penitent acts can make us righteous; we are righteous because of the Righteous One who lives in us Who forever took the punishment for our sin and shame on that cruel cross.

His Word also says, "There is therefore now no condemnation to them that are in Christ who walk not after the flesh, but after the Spirit" (Rom. 8:1). That settles it once and for all. The more we focus on what HE has done and not what WE have done, the more we will overcome sin and temptation in this life.

If the enemy or as the Bible calls him, "The accuser of the brethren," keeps telling you that you are a no good sinner and you don't deserve God's grace because of all that you have done wrong, tell him "you're a liar devil!" The Word says I am "made the righteousness of God in Christ" (2 Cor. 5:21) and therefore, I qualify for the blessing of Abraham!

One of the greatest benefits of being declared righteous by God, is the blessing of reconciliation and access into God's holy presence. The Psalmist David spoke about this in Psalm 24 and it's worth taking a look at for a moment as it further defines this amazing truth.

In Psalm 24, the Psalmist David is having a glorious revelation of THE Christ, the King of Glory. He is caught up in the wonder of His person, His being, His presence, and His glory. He is being blessed in the presence of the Lord.

Some scholars believe that he is seeing prophetically, hundreds of years before it actually happened, a vision of the Lord Jesus, riding triumphantly into the city of Jerusalem ... what we now refer to and celebrate as Palm Sunday. Christ, the triumphant King of kings, rightfully receiving shouts of exultation and praise from the very ones who would shortly cry out, "Crucify Him, crucify Him."

Still others believe that he is seeing the resurrected Lord, entering into heaven and taking His seat at the right hand of the Father having completed His work: the redemption of mankind. The very angels cry out as they witness the divine processional, "Who is this King of Glory?" They fold their wings and bow at the brightness of His being crying "Holy, holy, holy."

One thing is certain … David is captivated by what he is seeing and perhaps, caught up in a heavenly trance or is experiencing what is known in theological definition as a theophany — a pre-incarnate appearance of Christ. There are many examples in the Old Testament in which the Lord, Himself, appeared to men and spoke to them hundreds of years prior to His birth in a manger. In each case, that person's life was never the same because of the Divine encounter, and the very course of their life was altered forever. Examples like Moses and the burning bush in Exodus 3; Jacob wrestling with the Angel in Genesis 32; and the Lord appearing to Abram in Genesis 17 are just such examples and occasions recorded for us in the Bible. In each case, those who experienced such an encounter with the Lord were transformed and their lives were blessed as never before.

The impact of Abram's encounter not only affected him, his family, and their generations, but it is still affecting us today! We literally can enjoy and participate in the blessing of Abraham although hundreds of years have passed. In fact, the purpose of this book is to help you realize that the blessing is for you and me today and is available to all who believe.

The words of David are recorded in verse 3 of Psalm 24, which declare, "Who shall ascend into the hill of the Lord? Or who shall stand in His holy place?" I believe what he is really asking is this: who can have access into the presence of God? Who can go into God's holy presence? Who can experience the Shekinah glory of God? Who is eligible or who qualifies to have an audience in God's holy presence and glory? He answers the question in verse 4 when he says, "He that has clean hands and a pure heart; who has not lifted up his soul unto vanity, nor sworn deceitfully." (vs 5) "He [in other words, the righteous man he has just mentioned in verse 4] shall receive the blessing from the Lord, and righteousness from the God of his salvation."

Grace Sufficient For All

This might be cause for discouragement knowing that it is impossible for any of us to meet this requirement as our "righteousness is as filthy rags" and no matter how hard we try, we are going to "fall short of the glory of God" and fail. You've most likely heard the expression "He or she fell from grace," often referring to a believer who fell into sin. Actually, we as Christ followers and believers shouldn't fall FROM grace; we should fall TO grace.

Corrie ten Boom, the well-known author of **The Hiding Place**, a book about her family's experience during World War II in which they hid Jews in their attic from the Nazi's but eventually were discovered and brought to the concentration camp, used to say, "There isn't a pit too deep that His love isn't deeper still." Regardless of how bad we may have messed up or failed the Lord, God's Word promised that, "His grace is sufficient" meaning that there is nothing that is out of the reach of His grace. Our tendency, like Adam and Eve in the Garden of Eden, is to hide when we have failed the Lord. Yet, we should do the opposite, for that is what He desires. We should run to Him and we will find Him with arms open wide to receive us back into the family, just like the prodigal son's Father welcomed him back after his detour into rebellion and disobedience.

The good news is, Paul tells us, "We have this treasure [the Spirit of the Lord] in earthen vessels" (2 Cor. 4:7) or in other words, while the gift or treasure that is inside us is perfect and righteous, the container, the temple in which He lives, is not. Only the Spirit of the Lord, the Righteous One, was tempted, as we are but did not yield to temptation to it and it is HE in us that makes us righteous (2 Cor. 2:15) fulfilling the conditions of Psalm 24: 3-4 which are requisite for the presence of God! Praise God! Actually, only HE, the Lord Jesus, is the ONE by whom we have access into the presence of the Father; we are accepted in the Beloved, Jesus the Son of God.

The Breath of His Spirit

Let me remind you of what David said in verse 5 of Psalms 24. "He shall receive the blessing from the Lord and righteousness from the God of his salvation." I believe the blessing He (the Lord) is referring to is related to the question He originally asked in verse 3 of the same Psalm. The blessing is access into His glorious presence on a continual basis ... the very breath of God, breathing into your life and spirit, quickening (making alive) you and me just as He did to Abraham centuries ago. It is made available to us, the children of Abraham, by the Holy Spirit. Paul describes it in Galatians 3:14: "That the blessing of Abraham might come on the Gentiles through Jesus Christ; that we might receive the promise of the Spirit through faith." In other words, Paul is saying to the saints in Galatia ... at least many of which were gentiles ... in a New Testament church, that the same Spirit of the Lord that visited Abraham (the father of the Israelites or the Jews) way back in Genesis 17 in the Old Testament, is the same Holy Spirit that rested on those that were gathered in the upper room after Christ ascended into heaven ... the same Spirit that blew like a mighty rushing wind into their hearts, baptizing them (Acts 2:4).

If you look at the derivation of the word "blessing" in the Hebrew language, you will find that one of the letter/words that make up this word blessing is in fact, the very same word hey, the 5th letter of the Hebrew alphabet. That same letter was inserted into Abram's name, making him Abraham, and also breathed life into him and his wife, Sarah.

David, in my opinion, had a revelation of this truth and was being blessed by his encounter in God's presence in Psalm 24. I'm comforted also in the fact that David, although he had a love for the Lord and heart after God's own heart, often failed miserably and was subject to the same tendency to succumb to the demands of the flesh as we are today. However, he was quick to repent and when he did, he once again was restored and reconciled to God's favor and blessing ... the presence of God's Spirit. Salvation, righteousness, reconciliation and access to God's presence are all yours and mine as children of Abraham and inheritors of the blessing of Abraham!

CHAPTER FIVE

The Blessing of Health and Healing

You may have heard statements such as this with regard to a prolonged illness or infirmity that a Christian in your church or your family has had to endure: "It's a blessing in disguise." Or perhaps you've heard something like this: "The Lord wants to teach me a lesson through the sickness I'm dealing with." While I agree that we can learn to trust the Lord to give us grace while we wait for healing, I must disagree emphatically with the premise that it is a blessing or that the illness came from God in the first place! Make no mistake about it … sickness is part of the curse that came from the fall of man back in the Garden of Eden and more importantly, part of what our precious Savior came to destroy on Calvary (Gal. 3:13). Not to be harsh or unfeeling, but some of the very same people who say things like "this is God's will for me" go to their doctor for treatment and take the prescribed medicines to be "cured" of that very same sickness.

If sickness is "from" God, then is it not disobedience to God in trying to seek help to have it cured? No, my friend, that's not the nature of our God nor does this kind of thinking line up with the Word of God. Am I saying that if you are sick or if a loved one of yours died from an illness, they were not believers or they did not have enough faith to believe God for their miracle? Absolutely not! My own precious Dad who was a man of faith like few men I have known in my life, died of congestive heart failure at age 71 despite believing God for his healing. Sometimes in God's omniscience and sovereignty, He chooses to take one of His children home for reasons that are beyond our understanding. In those instances we must trust Him and understand that we only "see in part" as the scripture says.

However, I believe that for the most part, it is God's desire and will for us to not only be healed when we do become sick but to believe and trust Him for divine health and a long life.

A Father's Heart

I have been a father for over 26 years now and I can tell you without a moment's hesitation that there is no way I would ever inflict my son with a deadly disease or cause him harm deliberately to "teach him a lesson." The Bible says we are made in the image of God and after His likeness (Gen. 1:27). My innate desire to protect and spare my child from pain or anything that would try to hurt him comes from the fact that I have a heart like the Heavenly Father's heart. The Heavenly Father's heart was not only to redeem His creation from sin that separated him from fellowship and communion but also to heal him from the dreadful results of sin which brought sickness and pain into the world. He Himself said in Ex. 15:26, " I AM the Lord that heals you." He was saying my very nature is to be a Healer! The above referenced verse, Galatians 3:13, says clearly what Christ was sent to accomplish on the Cross. "Christ has redeemed us from the curse of the law, having become a curse for us (for it is written, "Cursed is everyone who hangs on a tree." Sickness is part of the curse that Jesus redeemed [paid for] for us on the cross. If Jesus already took care of it on the cross, why should we then carry it or bare it in our bodies? There are many more scriptures, some of which I will give you later in this chapter that state clearly that Jesus paid with the shedding of His very own blood, the price for you and me to be healed, and healing is definitely part of the atonement. I believe that is why He raised up great men and women in our day and has also allowed me the privilege to preach this truth and help God's people believe for all that is provided for them as part of the blessing Jesus paid for.

The well known healing evangelist, the late Oral Roberts, told the story of a man who approached him in one of his services. The man evidently did not believe in healing and as much as said so. Oral's reply was priceless. He asked the man to give him his Bible. The man handed his Bible to him. Dr. Roberts accepted the Bible and asked the man to bring him a scissors. The man looked at him with a puzzled expression on his face and said something to the effect of, "What for?"

Oral then replied, "You say you don't believe in healing. Well, I'm going to cut every verse about healing out of the Bible since you don't believe it's God's will to heal." The man objected emphatically and said, "That would be destroying the Bible!" Oral wisely replied, "That's exactly what you do when you say that God does not heal today ... you destroy the Word of God!" Oral was exactly right! Anyone who has studied the Word of God with diligence knows that there is no way you can come to conclusion that it is not God's desire to heal and that He made every provision for it in sending His Son, Jesus, to pay the price for our healing.

As mentioned earlier, I worked for many years with Pastor Benny Hinn, a noted healing evangelist. In hundreds of services over the 22 years that I worked with him full time, when people were led into worship, the Lord's presence became very real and there was a release of the anointing or the miraculous power of God, and many received healing in their bodies. You will NEVER convince me that God does not heal today! These eyes have seen too many get healed, too many miracles to ever believe that lie! I praise God that now the same kinds of supernatural demonstrations are now occurring in my own meetings as I have traveled the world since January of 2010.

Miracle In Bogota

In September of 2013, I was invited to preach in Bogota, Columbia. After preaching a powerful message, we entered a time of worship. When Jesus becomes real to those in attendance and their faith rises to believe that He is greater than the sickness that may be plaguing their body, many get healed right then and there. As often is the case, the Holy Spirit began to give me Words of Knowledge of people that were being held of various illnesses. I received a Word of Knowledge that a woman was being healed of a tumor on her breast. I gave the word, but at first, there was no response. For a brief moment I thought to myself, "Well Jim, you must have missed it on that one … maybe that was just your mind and not the Spirit of the Lord speaking." But then, I quickly dismissed that thought because I have learned to trust in the accuracy of the Word of Knowledge. I gave the Word again, but there was still no response. I was about to move on when I gave the Word a third time. Then, a woman, a pastor's wife, who had been sitting right in front of me on the front row of the audience, motioned to me that she was the one being healed of the tumor. She had been afraid to step out but then her daughter encouraged her to step forward. The moment she stepped out of her seat, the Lord healed her. Praise His Name forever!

When she came up on the platform, I asked her about it and she began to describe the problem. The Lord further instructed me to tell her that the pain would leave immediately and that in a few days, the lump would disappear. That is exactly what happened! The pain immediately left her body, and the next morning when she came back for the morning service, she couldn't wait to testify that there was no trace of the tumor on her breast! Glory to God!

This was the direct result of what happens when someone experiences the power of God for healing which is part of the blessing of Abraham. When He breathes on your life, your body or whatever part of your life that needs healing, His power will touch you and make you whole! Glory to His mighty Name! By the way, last year in 2014 I returned to that same church in Bogota again, and I saw this dear woman and she is still healed!

This is just one of the many testimonies of healing that demonstrates that the blessing of health and healing is one of the benefits of the blessing of Abraham that can affect our lives on a daily basis as we walk in divine health and experience divine healing in times of need. Healing is a work of the Spirit of the Lord! It is the will of the Father, purchased by the Son and performed in us by the Holy Spirit. As one raised in a home where God's healing power was always recognized, I grew up watching my Mom and my Dad trust God for their health and healing, and as a result, it has always been part of my spiritual heritage and what I believe.

Divine health and healing are part of the blessing of Abraham. One of the most salient facts and truths about the Blessing of Abraham, which we have now established, transpired when the "hey" of the Spirit of the Lord (the breath of God) breathed into his body as recorded in Genesis 17:5, and Abraham and his wife Sarah were healed as a result of that divine exhalation!

Their once aged bodies … well past childbearing years … were quickened (made alive) and healed, becoming like the bodies of a young man and woman able to reproduce and have a child.

One of my favorite verses in Scripture has long been Romans 8:11 which tells us that the Spirit of the Lord is a quickening or healing Spirit. "But if the Spirit of Him who raised Jesus from the dead dwells in you, He who raised Christ from the dead will also give life to your mortal bodies through His Spirit who dwells in you" (Rom 8:11).

The Same Spirit

This verse makes clear a couple of powerful truths about the Spirit of the Lord who is living in us. Notice it says, "If the Spirit of Him who raised Jesus from the dead..." It was the Holy Spirit that raised Jesus' body from the dead. Healing is a work of the Spirit of the Lord! The Father included it in His will for us, the Son purchased it with His stripes on Calvary, and the Holy Spirit transfers or performs it when our bodies need to be healed. The mystery of the Trinity is seen here and it clearly states that without the intervention and cooperation of the Holy Spirit, Christ's resurrection would not have happened. Jesus, who was very much God, became very much man so as to identify with our fallen human state. Furthermore, Jesus was dependent on the Holy Spirit to perform the miracles He did during His three years of ministry on earth after His baptism and when the hour would come, to raise Him from the dead.

Accordingly, as part of our inheritance, we have the same promise of the Spirit (Gal. 3:14) living and breathing in our bodies and it will in the same manner heal and restore health to us when sickness and disease threaten to rob us and impair the quality of our lives.

God's Healing Power ... From Generation to Generation

My dear Mom, who is now with Jesus, stood on this verse countless times throughout her almost 87 years of life as she needed healing many times, even as an infant. My Mom, who was also a twin as I am, became very weak and ill after her twin sister, Marie, passed away at the age of one. Being a twin myself, I can tell you that twins share a bond that is very strong right from the womb and when something happens to your twin, it affects you also.

My Mom mourned the loss of her twin for about one year, even though she was too young to be conscious of it. She literally stopped eating which, of course, caused her body to become weak and frail. She almost passed away herself but God had a plan for not only her life, but for mine and my brothers' lives and answered the prayers of my godly grandparents and restored her young life back to health. I'm told that my Mom's aunt, whom we affectionately called "Aunt Jin" (short for Jeanette) who lived with them as she had been orphaned when my Mom's grandparents both died, fed my Mom small pieces of Hershey's chocolate bars because that was the only thing she would eat for weeks, and it kept her alive. So you see, right from the start, my Mom's life would need the Spirit of the Lord to heal her and raise her up back to health.

Another time, when I was a small boy, I remember her telling us that the doctors had told her that she had a cyst the size of a grapefruit and it was life threatening. My Mom stood on the many healing scriptures in the

Word and miraculously, the cyst disappeared and she was made whole. Another time she went blind temporarily, but she and my Dad understood that healing is our inheritance and part of the blessing that was purchased for us, and it wasn't long before her sight returned and she could once again to care for us, her four young boys.

I believe this is why in large part, she had an affinity for healing ministries and was a follower of T.L. Osborne, Oral Roberts, Kathryn Kuhlman and read every book she could find on healing such as the classic Christ the Healer by F. F. Bosworth. I remember her telling me about the miraculous healing testimony of Betty Baxter, the story of a woman whose body had been twisted, crippled and deformed, having been born with a curve in her spine which caused every vertebra to be out of place, with the bones twisted and matted together. Her condition worsened, causing momentary blindness and deafness, with an ongoing state of total immobility. Yet, this same young girl was miraculously healed when the Spirit of the Lord entered her bedroom on a previously prophesied day. So, healing was very much a common thing in our household, and although we believed in doctors, the first one we consulted when sickness struck, was the Great Physician, Jesus! In the providence of God, her son would one day work with and travel the world with what was arguably one of the largest healing ministries ever and be privileged to see many people healed by God's power. In the last few years of her life, she was so thrilled to see me minister in healing in my own meetings and always was eager to hear the testimonies of those that were healed by God's power when I would call her upon returning from a ministry trip.

The Power of The Spoken Word

Psalm 107:20 says, "He sent His word and healed them, And delivered them from their destructions." The Word of God is not like a boomerang that goes out and then comes back, accomplishing nothing. No, Isaiah 55:11 say, "So shall my Word be that goes forth out of My mouth; it shall not return unto me void, but it shall accomplish what I please and it shall prosper in the thing for which I sent it." No, the Word is like a divine arrow that goes expressly to where the Spirit of the Lord sends it and ALWAYS hits its target or mark to accomplish God's will. This is why we should use the Word when we pray, speaking it out of our mouths with faith and expect a return on it. Amen!

Think about that for a moment! It is impossible to speak God's Word out of your mouth and not have it accomplish something! Wow! That something may not be seen in the natural realm, but none-the-less, something has transpired in the spiritual realm and it's just a matter of time before it will be seen!

However, let me say at this point that it's not mere recitation of the Word of God that brings divine results of healing. When the anointing of God's Spirit breathes on you and makes the Word of God and specifically a particular scripture real and life to you, that's the time to speak it out of your mouth and believe for your healing!

Healing and Health For The Believer

One of the reasons God sent His Son, Jesus, was to do exactly that: to heal. Healing was very much on the mind of God the Father, God the Son, and God the

Holy Spirit and so after a heavenly conference, the plan for salvation and healing was laid out and the Son of God was dispatched to earth to carry it out. We sing in one of our favorite Christmas Carols, "Christ the Savior is born" and indeed He was born in a manger long ago. We could also sing "Christ, the Healer is born" because healing is part of His very nature; He's a healing Jesus and one of His names, "Jehovah Rophe," means the Lord Who heals! When His Spirit comes to live inside us, healing and health come as well! Healing is the bi-product of His presence living and breathing in us.

In fact, if you study the Greek word "sozo" from which we get the English word salvation in the New Testament (which was originally translated from the Greek), you discover that it means salvation for the total man … body, soul and spirit. As part of the abundant life that John 10:10 says He came to bring us, divine healing and health are ours in Christ Jesus.

Our Present-Day Promise

One of the most quoted passages of scripture on healing is found in Isaiah 53: 4-5, which says: "Surely He has borne our griefs and carried our sorrows; Yet we esteemed Him stricken, smitten by God, and afflicted. 5 But He was wounded for our transgressions, He was bruised for our iniquities; The chastisement for our peace was upon Him, And by His stripes we are healed" (Is. 53:4-5, NKJV). Isaiah's prophecy reached down through the centuries to when Jesus, the Savior and Healer, would live and die, forever purchasing salvation and healing for us today.

I love the fact that Isaiah begins with the word "surely!" Isaiah 53:4 says, "Surely ..." This word "surely" in the Hebrew language, the original language of the Old Testament, is a strong word which denotes an unwavering stance on the truth he is about to declare. Not maybe, or hopefully but absolutely, positively, definitely, He has born our griefs! The word "griefs" is more accurately translated "sickness" and in some translations of the Bible you will see it used instead of griefs. He goes on to say in that verse "and carried our sorrows." The word "sorrows" is more accurately translated "pains". Unmistakably, the prophet states that He, Jesus, bore our sicknesses and our pains when He died on the cross. He took them so that you and I would not have to bare them. If we are carrying sickness and pain, we need to remember the words of the prophet Isaiah and stand on them in faith for our healing. Today, no matter what has come against your body, agree with Isaiah the prophet and say it without doubt or hesitation as he did, "Surely ... He has borne my sickness and carried my pain!"

The prophet Isaiah goes on to say in verse 5 "and by His stripes we are healed!" We ARE healed ... a present tense, timeless, never-ending promise to you and me! The stripes that Jesus took on His back were for the healing of our sicknesses, diseases and pain. I believe that with every stripe He bore on His back, He paid for every possible category of disease and sickness known to man.

Believe Isaiah's prophetic declaration about Jesus' perfect and finished work for you and speak these healing words over your body or over the body of a loved one or friend in need of healing … by His stripes we are healed.

Healed in His Presence

Another example of this is seen in Luke 5:17. "Now it happened on a certain day, as He was teaching, that there were Pharisees and teachers of the law sitting by, who had come out of every town of Galilee, Judea, and Jerusalem. And the power of the Lord was present to heal them." Notice this verse says, "It happened [healing] … as He was teaching, the power of the Lord was present to heal them. In other words, as Jesus' words were leaving His mouth, those who were in the crowd that had gathered were being healed that very moment. I love that! The Word of God is powerful! He didn't even have to lay hands on them, and they were receiving healing! Miracles were the direct result of His powerful words!

Hebrews 13:8 says, "Jesus Christ is the same yesterday, today, and forever." Jesus hasn't changed, nor will He ever change! If He healed back then, He heals today! If His Word healed them as they listened to Him speak, it still heals today when it is spoken or read. I often tell people when I minister, don't wait for the end of the service to be healed or for me to lay hands on you to receive a healing touch for your body. Just as the Spirit of the Lord healed the people who gathered in Luke 5:17 as Jesus spoke, so today, when a man or woman of God who is filled with the Spirit of the Lord preaches the Word of God, you can be healed as it is going forth! If the preacher is truly anointed by the Holy Spirit, it's not the man speaking (or woman) … it's the Spirit of the Lord speaking under the anointing and the power of the Word is present to heal. I have had many testify after I preached that while they were listening to the message, they received their healing. Hallelujah! "Jesus Christ, the same, yesterday, today and forever!" (Heb. 13:8). Amen!

The Power of The Word to Heal

As an example of what I have just said, I recently ministered at a church in the Dayton, Ohio area. I preached a message entitled "The Blood Speaks" based on Hebrews 12:24 which states that the blood of Jesus speaks better things. One of the points of my message is that it speaks healing to us today. I sensed a strong anointing on me as I preached and after the message, began ministering in healing. Shortly into this segment of the service, I notice a woman who was walking very slowly from the back of the auditorium assisted by a younger lady who I later found out was her daughter. It was obvious that every step was an effort and that she was in tremendous pain. When she got to the altar I asked her what her name was and she replied, "Stephanie." I then asked her what was wrong and why she had come forward. Sometimes the Holy Spirit will give me Words of Knowledge that certain sicknesses are being healed but at other times, as in the case of Stephanie, I just ask them what is wrong or what they are believing for. Stephanie began to tell me and the audience that several weeks earlier, she had moved a certain way and her back literally broke. From that moment on she had been experiencing excruciating pain and was, in fact, in terrible pain at the moment she was speaking to me. I asked her if she believed that the Lord could and would heal her and she said, "Definitely!" I do that because I believe that it's important to know whether the person you are about to pray for is in agreement with the Word that says, "I Am the Lord that heals You," and am in agreement with you for healing when you pray.

I laid hands on her back and felt a steel brace running from her neck all the way down to her lower back which, up until then, I hadn't noticed because it was covered by her sweater. We prayed and in an instant she was completely relieved of the horrible pain she had just moments earlier! I said, "Take that brace off!" I encouraged to do so as an act of faith. She began undoing the snaps and straps that tightly held her spine. When she had finished undoing the snaps, she removed the brace and lifted it up, walking all over with hands raised praising the Lord as she exclaimed "I have no pain….I have no pain!" In that miraculous moment, Stephanie experienced her healing which is part of the blessing we have received through Christ's death on the cross. "With His stripes we are healed." You see, the cross, transfers the blessing to us … the same healing power that breathed life into Abraham and Sarah's bodies had been breathed into Stephanie's body, healing her broken back. By the way, the pastor of that church has emailed me several times to say that Stephanie is still healed and as a result of her healing, she brought four family members to church the following Sunday and they all accepted the Lord as their Savior! Praise the Lord! Healing is a sign to the unbeliever that He is Who He said He is and that His power is alive and well.

You can be healed right in your home as you agree with the Word of God and speak it out in faith for your healing. Remember that the Word of God is His Word to us recorded under the inspiration of the Holy Spirit to the various writers in both the Old and New Testaments. Ask the Holy Spirit to quicken your understanding as you read and meditate on it. Expect to be healed as the power of the Word becomes life and health to your body as Proverbs 4:22 states is will be.

Perhaps you are reading this book and you are dealing with a sickness in your body or a situation that no matter how you have prayed, seems to be immoveable or insurmountable? I encourage you right now to take a break from reading this book, get into God's presence by worship and prayer, and ask Him to breathe on your body His breath of life and restoring power. In fact, let me pray with you right here and now:

Prayer for Healing

"Father, in the Name of Jesus, Your Son, I agree with Your Word for healing for my brother or sister from this sickness and pain in their body. Your Word says in Isaiah 53:5, "By His stripes we ARE healed." We stand on Your Word, knowing it cannot lie and believe today for a miracle of divine intervention and supernatural power to quicken, make alive, heal that diseased or dead part of the reader's body, or marriage, or finances, or family member that has no room for God and perform a miracle like You did in Abram's and Sarai's bodies. Breathe your healing, creative power into them and make them whole right now. Amen." I know that you are being healed even as I am writing these words. To God be the glory!

Not only has God provided healing in the atonement, but I believe it is His will and plan that we live in health and avoid sickness and disease in the first place. How can I make a statement like that, you might ask? It is seen in passages of scripture in both the Old and New Testaments, that's how.

Verses like Proverbs 4:22 say, speaking of the Word of God, "For they are life to those who find them and health to one's whole body." The Word of God is God-breathed and just reading it or meditating on it can breathe health and life into your very being and body.

Did you know that the Word of God can actually add years to your life and make those years quality years of health, strength and productivity? Proverbs 3:1-2 says, "My son, forget not my law; but let thine heart keep my commandments: For length of days, and long life, and peace, shall they add to thee" (KJV).

Health and Long Life Promised

Length of days and long life are often assumed to be one and the same. Actually, they are not. Length of days is a reference to "how" your days will be or the quality of your days; in others that you will live in health, peace and prosperity and be more productive than those who ignore the principals of the Word of God.

Long life, on the other hand refers to "how many" years you will live. I believe that we as Christians should expect our years to be quality years full of health, strength and peace but also that we will live a long life. Why? So that we can do more for the Kingdom of Christ … reach more with the gospel of Jesus Christ … give more to the work of the Lord and so on.

Conversely, I believe that many Christian lives have been cut short because of not discerning the body of Christ which I believe is not realizing all that the work of the Lord on Calvary has provided for us, including divine health and healing.

As Spirit-filled believers, we must believe that the breath of the Spirit of God, the blessing of Abraham, has provided health and healing for our bodies and expect enjoy the benefits of not only a long life but also divine health and quality days all the days of our lives.

I pronounce these benefits of the blessing of Abraham over my life and my family often. May I suggest that you find some post-it notes and stick them on the refrigerator or in places that you will see them? Begin to speak them out of your mouth often.

Health and Healing declarations (adapted from Scripture to make them personal from the Word):

1. "with His stripes I am healed!" (Isa. 53:5)

2. "Your Word Lord, is life and health to my flesh. (Prov. 4:22)

3. "You are the God that heals me!" (Ex. 15:26)

4. "You sent Your Word and healed my disease!" (Ps. 107:20)

5. "Surely You have born my sickness and carried my pains … therefore I give them to you and agree for healing Jesus!" (Isa. 53:4)

6. Since the same Spirit that raised You, Jesus, from the dead, is living in me, You are quickening, making alive and healing my mortal body! (Romans 8:11)

7. Jesus took every curse of sickness (Gal. 3:13) on Him when He suffered the stripes on His back (Isa. 53:5) so that today, I walk in the blessing of divine health and healing from every disease. (Gal. 3:14) I will live a long, healthy life.

CHAPTER SIX

The Blessing of Peace...
The Shalom Blessing

John 20:21-22 says, "So Jesus said to them again, 'Peace be with you; as the Father has sent Me, I also send you.' And when He had said this, He breathed on them and said to them, 'Receive the Holy Spirit.'"

The Promise of Peace

Peace, my friend, is part of our inheritance as the children of Abraham. Whatever you are facing now, let the Lord breathe His peace into your being right now as you are reading this book and claim what's rightfully yours in Christ.

I don't think it's an accident that just before Jesus breathed on the disciples to receive the Holy Spirit, He *blessed* them with the words peace be with you. There is a strong correlation between the breath of God (the blessing of the Spirit) in your life and the realization of His perfect peace. The very presence of God's breath in you produces a peace that cannot be produced by any other means.

You have probably heard it taught, but just in case, let me point out that there are two types of peace that we receive when we accept and receive the Lord Jesus Christ into our hearts. They are: peace with God and the peace of God.

There Is No peace OF God Without Peace WITH God!

Peace with God is ours when we accept the perfect sacrifice of His Son, Jesus, on the Cross and believe on Him as our Savior. It is our righteous standing with God … our position in Christ that has been reconciled, restored and purchased by the blood of Jesus. It's the peace of knowing that all is well with our souls and our standing before God, and we no longer have to hide in fear of His judgment because the penalty has been paid in full by His Son and appropriated to our hearts through faith. The separation that was caused by man's sin in the Garden of Eden was reconciled when Jesus became our peace offering, when He willingly humbled Himself and became obedient to the cross. Philippians 2:8 says, "And being found in fashion as a man, he humbled himself, and became obedient unto death, even the death of the cross."

His Supreme act of humility paid the price for us to be brought near to God as Ephesians 2:13 tells us: "But now in Christ Jesus you who once were far off have been brought near by the blood of Christ" (**NKJV**).

The blood of Jesus brings us near to God … in other words, back into His glorious presence where there is no condemnation, no fear of judgment, no separation because of sin, thereby giving us peace with God.

However, as I said, there's also a second kind of peace that is ours as part of the blessing of Abraham. It becomes ours as a divine result of peace with God coming to our hearts: the peace of God. Without peace with God, it is impossible to experience the peace of God!

"Peace [shalom] I leave with you, my peace I give unto you: not as the world gives, give I unto you. Let not your heart be troubled, neither let it be afraid" (John 14:27).

When Jesus said these amazing words to the disciples, He had just finished teaching them about the Holy Spirit, the Comforter Whom He said He would ask the Father to give them after He would be taken up back into heaven to prepare a place for them. Here again, we see a strong correlation between the Holy Spirit's presence in the believer's life and the presence of peace. Peace is a fruit of His Spirit living in us. This word Shalom is a power-packed word! Let me share with you the revelation of what it means in the heart and life of you and me as Christians, or Christ followers.

Shalom – More Than a Greeting

There are a couple of observations I'd like to draw your attention to about the word peace (shalom) that the

Lord Jesus uses in this familiar passage of scripture. If you visit Israel, as I have on numerous occasions, you will often be greeted by the locals with the word "shalom." It is a common greeting used in much the same way as we here in the US say hello and good-bye or as the Italians say the word "ciao." (I had to throw that in there because of my Italian heritage.) However, it is actually much more than just a common greeting … much, much more in fact!

I have heard Rabbis and Hebrew scholars teach about this word "shalom" and even every day Orthodox Jews will tell you the same thing: when you say, "Peace," or "Shalom," the Hebrew word used here that Jesus spoke to them, you are pronouncing a blessing on that person and their entire family for that matter. The word peace isn't just a relaxed state of mind either, by any means! The word "shalom" means TOTAL well-being … not just your mind, but your body, soul, spirit and every facet of your life! When The Blessing of Abraham comes on your heart and life, you are truly blessed with the shalom blessing of His peace in your total man. No part of you is lacking or left unaffected by it because the Prince of Peace is living inside of you, breathing His blessing into every aspect of your life. This would include your marriage, your finances, your business dealings, your health also!

The Blessing of Abraham is part of your birthright as a believer in Christ Jesus and as a child of Abraham! In Hebrew tradition, the birthright was a blessing passed on from a father to his eldest male child just prior to his death. I will elaborate more on that later but for now, just know that it is part of your inheritance as the first born in Jesus Christ and is for you and your household and the generations that follow. We know that because Jesus said, "My peace I leave with you." The word leave here in Hebrew is the connotation of someone who bequeaths or leaves an estate or an inheritance to his loved ones after he or she passes. Jesus wants us to know, that He has left for us or bequeathed to us His Shalom blessing in every dimension of our life because the Comforter, the Holy Spirit, the Spirit of the Lord, is residing in us. I like to think of it this way: the Father left us His will, purchased by the Son and distributed by the Executor of the Will, the Holy Spirit. It's the Spirit of the Lord that blesses us with the shalom blessing of the Lord and imparts it to us as we need it.

In our household growing up, and even throughout our adult lives, we have often used the expression "all is well" when we were facing a trying or difficult situation that had presented itself and was challenging our faith. I believe it started after my Dad, who was a carpenter by trade, fell off of a steep roof and broke all of his ribs. Miraculously, his life was spared and interestingly enough, with the extra insurance money after the medical bills had been paid, he purchased a piano for my Mom who was a wonderful pianist. It was on that piano, that my twin brother John and me learned how to play the piano and which would eventually be the launching or our adult musical careers and ministry! When the incident happened, my Mom wondered where their income would come and how she was going to feed and clothe their four young growing boys. My Dad, who had great faith and who always possessed a disposition of peace, said to her…"don't worry Mom, all is well!" And you know what? It was! When one job would end, almost without fail, he'd get another call to begin a new one that would last for several weeks or month and the Lord provided over and over again in that manner. That little phrase, all is well stuck in the family and we used it over and over and often when we faced adversity as a family. We weren't being superficial or insincere, it was just our way of reminding each other, our faith was anchored in the fact that our Lord, Jesus' presence in our lives, family and household would see us through the storm and that in the end, His shalom peace and blessing would work everything out for our eventual good, no matter how bad things seemed now. We were saying shalom without using the word and pronouncing the blessing on each other and the circumstances at hand knowing the Prince of Peace would reign supreme over all the affairs of our lives.

What I'm about to share with you is very personal. However, I feel I must share it for those who may be going through a battle with fear, which is the adversary of God-given peace. I can say with confidence and from personal experience that there is a way out of your valley of despair, and God can and will bring you out victoriously.

Say Goodbye To Fear

There are a few things you must do to realize your victory. Your experience with the spirit of fear may not be as extreme as mine was, but all of us, no matter how long we have been in Christ, or no matter how strong we may appear on the outside, have had battles with fear to some degree. For those who may be dealing with it now, let my testimony be an encouragement to you that the Spirit of the Lord is greater than the spirit of fear. He will deliver you and bring you out by His power!

Back when I was a freshman in Bible College, I went through a devastating experience with fear that almost derailed my life and the ministry that the Lord had for me to accomplish. Without exaggeration, for a time I actually feared I was losing my mind, and the devil as much as whispered that lie often to me during that horrible season in my life. It seemed out of no where, I was attacked by a spirit of fear, and it literally crippled me to the point that I had to call my parents and ask them to come and get me and bring me home.

A Taste of His Presence

Prior to that, I had never experienced fear like this and had enjoyed a normal, happy childhood. I had the blessing of being born into a godly family with a heritage of faith and had been filled with the Holy Spirit at the age of twelve. In fact, my baptism in the Holy Spirit was so glorious that for hours afterward, I couldn't speak in English but spoke in the heavenly language that the Lord had given me. At the time, Pastor David DeMola, who is now the Pastor of the great church Faith Fellowship in Sayreville, New Jersey was an evangelist. He had come in 1968 to hold a revival at my home church in Nutley, New Jersey. During the two weeks of the revival, many of the young people in our church had been filled with the Holy Spirit. I was spiritually hungry to experience the same glory and infilling of the Holy Spirit, and

I was getting discouraged because it had not happened to me yet.

I remember clearly that on the Sunday morning — the last day of the revival — when Pastor DeMola gave the altar call for those who wanted to receive the baptism of the Holy Spirit, I went forward quickly with many of my fellow youth who prayed earnestly with me to receive. In that service, all of a sudden these foreign words began coming to my mind and I began to speak them out, though with some hesitation and faltering. Pastor DeMola, being very wise, counseled me not to be satisfied with that but to come back that night and prophetically spoke that the Lord would fill me to overflowing in the evening service. That is exactly what happened. I came back and once again, when the altar appeal was given, I went forward and began seeking the Lord with all my heart. Suddenly, I was overcome by the presence of the Spirit of the Lord and I began to praise and speak in a fluent language that continued for hours. It was as if a well of Living Water was erupting from deep within me … an experience that I will never forget! I was gloriously filled with the Spirit. It was then that I knew that my life had a calling on it for full time ministry and left for Zion Bible College just a few years later in 1972.

I remember how excited my twin brother, John, and I were when we arrived on campus in the fall of 1972 to begin our college life. Everything was going along great until, as I said earlier, this horrible attack began.

Ambushed By The Enemy

Then, suddenly my mind was attacked with the most vile, horrible thoughts and the enemy began to tell me viscous lies that literally shut me down and paralyzed me. He said things like, "You aren't really a Christian;" "You have blasphemed the Holy Ghost;" "You will never make it ministry;" "You will never be married or have children;" "You will end up committing suicide," and much worse things that I don't care to repeat. I was so devastated by it that I couldn't even think straight, let alone go to classes and continue studying. It comforted me years later to learn that other men of God who were called to impact the world, went through similar experiences. Satan will do everything he can to rob us of our peace and in so doing, try to thwart the plan of God for our lives. He's a liar and was defeated when Jesus cried "it is finished" and forever secured perfect peace for us that day on Calvary.

Thankfully, I had a Mom and Dad who understood spiritual warfare and came quickly to my aid. My Mom drove up to Rhode Island from New Jersey to pick me up and take me home for a while and they began teaching me how to stand against the wicked one and his lies; how to do battle in the spirit realm. I remember my Dad saying, "Jim, the devil is like a big dog who at first seems ferocious who is charging towards you. Most often, if you stand still, he will come up to you, sniff around a little and then run off because he will sense that you are not afraid of him." Not to say that the devil does not have power, but often times, "His bark is bigger than his bite," and the Word says he comes "as a roaring lion seeking whom he may devour" to scare us and put us in the bondage of fear. We must stand against him "in the power of His might" and the Word then declares, as we resist him, he will flee from us. This kind of resistance is not just a mental thing; it is only possible when the Spirit of the Lord lifts up a standard against him," (Isa. 59:19) and he realizes he's no match for the Lord!

Our Authority As Believers

My Mom spoke these powerful passages of scripture like the one I just referenced and many more like "No weapon formed against you shall prosper and every tongue that rises against you, thou shalt condemn" (Isa. 54:17), and 2 Corinthians 10:5, which says, "Casting down imagination and every high thing that exalts itself against the knowledge of God, and bringing into captivity every thought to the obedience of Christ" and that spirit of fear eventually left me.

Little by little, as I began to speak the Word of God and pray in the Spirit in the tongue He had given me several years earlier, I began to become stronger in my inner man and was able to resist the devil's wicked thoughts and lies and the peace of God began to fill my heart and mind. It was during this period as I spent time in the Lord's presence, He breathed overcoming power into my Spirit and it defeated the spirit of fear which had crippled me. It took several weeks but praise be to the Lord, I was able to not only go back to complete my Freshman year of college, but eventually graduated and even continued on to get my Bachelors' degrees in Music and in Bible Literature.

The Overcoming Power

From that time until now, it has never returned and I have learned that when you stand in your position of authority in Christ and use His Word, which is a mighty sword against the enemy, you become equipped with divine, supernatural strengthening and your heart is no longer fearful. Satan is a liar, my friend! It takes the breath of God's Spirit though to make the Word of God "rhema" to your Spirit and cause you to utilize your weapons of warfare against the enemy. By the way, just to shame the devil and prove him to be the liar that he is, that horrible experience was almost 40 years ago. Since then, I have now been in full time ministry for over 37 years, traveled millions of miles around the world, ministered in over 90 countries, stood in front of millions of people sharing the saving, healing gospel of Jesus Christ, have been married to my beautiful wife, Mindy for almost 30 years , and am a father of an awesome son, Daniel, who is now 26 and married to a lovely, Christian lady named Linsey. Take that, devil! I have experienced the blessing of peace that comes to your life when God's Spirit is living and breathing in you.

My friend, do not allow the spirit of fear to control you or destroy the abundant life that God has promised you as part of The Blessing of Abraham! Peace is part of your inheritance as a child of Abraham. The Lord left it for you when He said, "My peace give I unto you" (John 14:27), so take what is rightfully yours today.

In the forty years that have followed that horrible experience, I often used the lessons I learned during that time and know how to stand in the authority Christ has given us.

If I had succumbed to the spirit of fear and not realized my position in Christ Jesus, "far above all principality and powers" I would have forfeited an amazing tenure of ministry and many of the awesome blessings the Lord had in store me in my life.

Peace, Be Still!

Do you remember the New Testament story of when Jesus and the disciples got into a boat on the Sea of Galilee and a massive storm arose recorded for us in the gospel of Matthew 8:23–27 and Mark 4:35-41? The disciples began to panic and clamor, fretting for their lives and safety and what was the Lord doing? He was sleeping! Despite huge problem that had suddenly arisen, He was calmly sleeping in the boat as if oblivious to the situation. In response to their turmoil and their questioning, if He cared about their welfare, Jesus simply said, "Peace, Be Still!" How often we do the very same thing in reaction to the storms that come our way and Jesus' response is still the same to us today! When Jesus said these amazing words to the disciples, He was assuring them that He was aware of the crisis situation but to be still (or let him handle it) because His presence was with them, they could rest in knowing that as long as that was the case, everything was going to be alright in the end!

We read the account of this story in Mark 4: 35–41, which says, "On the same day, when evening had come, He said to them, 'Let us cross over to the other side.'

Now when they had left the multitude, they took Him along in the boat as He was. And other little boats were also with Him. And a great windstorm arose, and the waves beat into the boat, so that it was already filling. But He was in the stern, asleep on a pillow. And they awoke Him and said to Him, 'Teacher, do You not care that we are perishing?' Then He arose and rebuked the wind, and said to the sea, 'Peace, be still!' And the wind ceased and there was a great calm. But He said to them, 'Why are you so fearful? How is it that you have no faith?' And they feared exceedingly, and said to one another, 'Who can this be, that even the wind and the sea obey Him!'" (NKJV)

The word peace that Jesus uses when He rebuked the wind and the waves saying, "Peace, be still" is a different word for peace in Hebrew. It is the word *sintao* which means "be still or be quiet." He may not only have been speaking to the wind and the waves but also to disciples who were making a lot of noise in their frantic response to the violent storm rather than realizing that the One who controls the wind and the waves was in the boat with them and because of His presence, everything would turn out all right! How much like them are we when a crisis or a storm in life comes our way? Rather than trust in the fact that He, the Lord, is with us "in our boat" so to speak, right there with the authority over everything including sickness, death, hell and the grave, we panic and get ourselves all worked us into a frenzied state, even questioning as the disciples did when they asked, "Do You not care that we are perishing?"

That is why we must hide the Word of God in our hearts so that when the storms arise, when the difficult or even impossible situations come our way, the Holy Spirit can "bring back to our remembrance" the Truths of the Word and apply them to our hearts and minds, bringing perfect peace right there in the middle of the storm. Jesus has not left us defenseless; He left us the Blessing of Abraham, the promise of the Spirit (Gal. 3:14) to come to our aid in our moments of crisis. We can speak "peace, be still" to the storms of life, and they will subside just as the waves of the Sea of Galilee did at the sound of His voice and His command.

The Sea of Galilee

By the way, you might wonder when reading this famous passage as I did prior to my many tours of the Holy Land, how can a storm come up in minutes on the "sea" of Galilee when it's actually a huge lake? You see, that lake is situated beneath the intersection of two great mountain chains that form a wind tunnel which directly blows over the Sea of Galilee. When storms blow from the north, the wind picks up and is funneled down through the valley between those two mountains and literally in minutes, a gigantic storm can erupt on the Sea of Galilee. This is just one of the many, many examples of how visiting the Holy Land will breathe new life into your Bible reading and comprehension of how the geography and culture of the day give you understanding of the many things that Jesus taught and did in His earthly ministry.

One last thing that I'd like to bring your attention to before concluding this section on the Blessing of Peace is this. Notice that after Jesus said, "My peace I leave with you, My peace I give unto you," He said, "LET NOT your heart be troubled, neither LET it be afraid." The word let is a word of permission. In other words Jesus was saying you have the power to either give permission for fear to control your heart and mind and consequently your life, or to not let it do so by standing in your supernaturally given authority and power to speak to the storm as He did and command it to "be still." Remember that just as Jesus was with the disciples in their hour of need in that horrific storm on the Sea of Galilee, He is in you to provide His perfect shalom, total well-being to your mind, body, spirit and to every facet of your life, including your finances and relationships. He is with you also to speak "peace, be still" in your hour of despair.

Dear Reader, I encourage you to pause right now and speak to the storm in your life … that thing that tries to bring fear to your heart and mind … that tempest that assails you to take your eyes off the One who calms the storms in our lives: Jesus. The blessing of Peace is yours; it is part of your inheritance. As a child of God, take your place by faith and claim your inheritance today. As Jesus said, "Let not your heart be troubled, neither let it be afraid." Starting today, walk in the blessing of peace that is promised to you as a child of Abraham.

Remind yourself that you come from a heritage of faith and a long line of believers who have trusted in the God of our Father Abraham and just as He blessed them in every dimension of their lives with His Shalom peace, He will bless you also and the generations that follow you.

The Blessing of a Godly Heritage of Faith

"Blessed be the God and Father of our Lord Jesus Christ, which according to His abundant mercy has begotten us again into a lively hope by the resurrection of Jesus Christ from the dead, (vs 4) To an inheritance incorruptible, and undefiled, and that does not fade away, reserved in heaven for you." (1 Peter 1:3-4)

You might not think that you have a godly heritage because you were not brought up in a Christian home and you may be the only one in your family that you know of that is a believer. Actually, that is not the sole basis for defining a godly heritage, and I believe that by the time you finish reading this chapter, you will realize that you actually belong to a long line of faith as a child of Abraham.

In both my wife and my cases, we were blessed to have a legacy of faith and were born into Christian families; my heritage goes back over 100 years. I don't say this in a prideful manner but rather as an acknowledgement and an expression of immeasurable appreciation to the Lord for allowing me this privilege of a Christian lineage that began several generations ago.

My Heritage

My grandfather on my Mom's side, Grandpa Tarantino, came to the knowledge of the Lord and accepted Him as Savior shortly after immigrating to the United States from Italy around the turn of the last century. His brother had come to the US several years earlier and had become a born again, Spirit-filled Christian and subsequently was called into the ministry. He became a "sponsor" for my grandfather to be able to come to America, because in those days you had to have someone, usually a family member, as your sponsor financially and otherwise, as well as the promise of a job to support yourself. My grandfather's brother witnessed to him and led him to the Lord, and after he received salvation through his brother's witness, he became a preacher also. The two of them were "circuit preachers" as they were called back then and travelled around to the neighboring cities, establishing churches and preaching the gospel with power!

Those days were not easy for immigrants to the US, especially if you came from European extraction and countries such as Italy, Poland, Ireland, etc. Coupled with the fact that they became "Pentecostals," I'm told that they were doubly persecuted not only for their ethnicity but also for their faith. However, the faith instilled in them was born of the Holy Spirit and breathed overcoming, preserving power into them, making them mighty men of God!

One of the towns that they ministered in was the town of Belleville, the next town over from Nutley where my Mom's family had settled and where my Dad's mother, Grandma Cernero, had settled with her children. Her husband, my Grandpa Cernero, sadly had died of pneumonia just one month prior to my Dad's birth so my Dad never knew his earthly father, and we did not have the blessing on knowing him here on earth … we will one day though! I'm told that was in part, through the ministry of my Mom's dad, Grandpa Tarantino, that Grandma and Grandpa Cernero became born again believers and converted from Catholicism also. My Dad's eldest brother Felix, who was the only one of his siblings who was born in Italy, had come to America as a small boy and grew to be an awesome man of God. In the absence of their father, he became a father figure to my Dad, Nunziante and his brothers, Angelo, Francis, Joseph and their sister, Margarita. Uncle Felix had great faith and had a profound impact and influence on my Dad who in turn became a man of rock solid faith in the Lord Jesus Christ.

A Foundation of Faith

Grandpa Tarantino was a mighty man of God and a man of the Spirit. He was used by the Lord to cast out demons, pray for healing for the sick, and bring many to Christ. I'm very honored that some of my relatives say I remind them of him when I minister, and in fact, I resemble him in appearance as well.

Grandma Tarantino — my Mom's mother — was the only one of my grandparents who was not born in Italy, but was born in my home town of Nutley, New Jersey The story of her conversion to Christ is quite remarkable, in fact!

The Power of Praise and Worship

Grandma Tarantino was a very beautiful woman and always "dressed to the nines" (a popular expression I'm told in those days that meant you knew how to dress) as she would say. One day as the story goes, when she was in her late teens and prior to her getting saved, she walked to a local school to attend a dance where she was to meet her date. She was "all dolled up" and "bedoogled " (her made up word) with long gloves, a hat, and a dress like the "flappers" (dancers of the roaring twenties) she would say as she recounted the story to us her grandchildren. Well, believe it or not, her date stood her up and was a "no show." So, rather than hang around, she decided to leave and go back home. Providentially, on the way home, she passed by a Pentecostal church not far from where her family lived and as she was going by, she heard them singing joyously. Being quite musical herself with a lovely soprano voice, she was drawn into the building to check it out. Of course we realize looking back that it wasn't just the music that drew her into the church; it was the Holy Spirit Himself! As it "happens," my Grandfather was preaching that day and when he gave the altar call, my Grandmother recognized her need of the Lord and salvation and responded by going forward and accepting Him! She was gloriously saved that day and filled with the baptism of the Holy Spirit! Praise the Lord! As if that wasn't good enough, the Holy Spirit spoke to my Grandpa and said to him, "This will be your wife." I'm sure he was very pleased to hear those words from the Lord because she was beautiful!

A Godly Heritage

Soon after, they were married, and together, they served the Lord in ministry for many years. God soon blessed them with twin girls, Rachel, my Mom and her twin sister Marie, as well another daughter, my Aunt Esther and lastly a son, my Uncle Tom. Sadly, Marie died at age one and my Mom almost did a year later because of mourning her twin. Despite that terrible loss, their faith in the Lord remained steadfast and the blessing of the Lord was on them. In fact, I remember my grandmother telling us that several years after her conversion, the local Catholic priest came to "bless the house"(a tradition that was common in the Catholic Church in those days) and when my grandmother answered the door, she said, "Thank you, Father but that won't be necessary … our house is already blessed because we know the Lord!" He wasn't too happy and walked away rather abruptly. She meant him no disrespect, but Grandma was aware that when the Spirit of the Lord comes into your heart and life and He breathes in you His divine breath, every aspect of your life, including your finances and home, are blessed! If you are of the Catholic faith and reading my book, my intention is not to be insulting in any way, but only to tell the story as it happened, and in so doing, to demonstrate just how real the faith of my grandparents was after they received salvation.

Grandpa Tarantino worked as a brick mason in addition to his lay ministry and they were the first one's on Milton Avenue in Nutley to have modern appliances such as a washing machine, electric iron, telephone and a television. When the Spirit of the Lord comes into your life, along with His presence is fullness and abundance in every dimension! He's the Spirit of Grace! Another word for grace is favor, and both rested upon my grandfather and grandmother!

As I mentioned earlier in this chapter, Grandpa Tarantino and his brother started several churches and as my Mom grew and became a wonderful pianist and soprano singer, she would accompany him and play the piano for his services. Mom also played for her cousins, "The Tarantino Trio," who sang on the radio … a very big deal in those days! We would later tease Mom that she was famous. It was while accompanying my grandfather that my Mom met my Dad, fell in love and would eventually marry him after he returned from World War II. I'm told that the church held prayer meetings every night for the entire length of the war, praying for many men in the church, including my Dad, who were away serving in the war and that not one of those men were killed but returned home safely after the war. There's power in prayer!

A Mother's Prayer

I remember Mom telling us that although she and my Dad wanted children very badly, for several years after they married she failed to get pregnant. She would cry when she would see my cousins because she so desperately wanted children. She would often cry out to the Lord in prayer and say, "If You'll give us children, we will dedicate them to You and raise them to serve You all of their lives." The Lord heard that prayer! He eventually gave them four sons, my brother Tom, the eldest, then my brother Mark and then my twin brother, John and me. Three of us would become full time ministers of the gospel. Dad would often say, "I pray, Lord, that You will send them to the four corners of the earth" and the Lord heard that prophetic prayer as well! My brothers have each traveled to many countries in ministry. Because of my being on staff with Pastor Benny for more than two decades and now in my own ministry preaching since January of 2010 in many countries also, I have been to over 92 countries preaching and leading worship around the globe. To God be the glory! When the blessing is on your life, even the desires of your heart will match His, and He will answer your prophetic prayers in a manner that is beyond what you could have imagined! (Eph. 3:20)

A Century of Favor

So you can see why I say I am blessed to have a heritage in Christ that goes back approximately 100 years … a heritage that spans a full century! A family that although it had it's trials and tribulations just like everyone else and is far from perfect, yet my family knew that the Lord was their answer and He's the One they called on first in times of crisis. My grandparents' first language was Italian, and when they would pray, they would end their prayer in the "nome di Gesu" or "in the Name of Jesus." When we got sick or hurt as kids, we would tell Mom to call Grandpa Tarantino because we knew that if he prayed for us, we would soon be better … and we were!

My father's brother, our Uncle Angelo, also became a preacher of the gospel and when I was a young boy, we attended his church in Newark, New Jersey. I am grateful to Uncle Angelo and Aunt Margaret for their contribution as well to my growing in the knowledge of the Lord, and it was he that baptized me and my twin brother, John, in water in 1963 at the age of 9 years old. What a blessing to have had my Grandfather, Rev. Thomas Tarantino, there to not only witness our baptism but pray over us and impart his anointing on us as well at an early age! I am a believer in impartation … not just for those who are in full-time ministry, but every godly parent to their children and to the generations that follow. I believe strongly that the impartation I received that day as Grandpa prayed opened the blessing on my life for ministry and just a few years later, just prior to his death in February of 1968, I received the baptism of the Holy Spirit in a powerful way and simultaneously my calling to full time ministry.

I speak more in depth about my baptism in the Holy Spirit in chapter 14 titled "The Blessing of Another Spirit," but for now, I will just say it was a pivotal crossroad in my spiritual life where the Spirit of the Lord breathed into my heart and cemented my destiny in ministry. If you have not been filled with the Spirit and received the baptism of the Holy Spirit, I urge you ask Him to fill you right now! It is a free gift to all believers and yes, part of the blessing of Abraham, the same Spirit that breathed into his body will breathe into your heart and life. He will give you a heavenly language to pray with and give you power to witness and live an overcoming life. I say this often to young people when I preach, "You will find your destiny, your calling in life … in the presence of the Lord," and I believe that with all my heart. I also believe that as we continue to serve the Lord and grow in the knowledge of the Lord, He will "enlarge our territory" or our sphere of influence for His Kingdom when we spend time waiting on Him in His glorious presence.

I know that many of you reading this book may not have had the blessing of being born biologically into a godly, Christian family as I was and may feel as though you don't have a heritage of faith. Actually, that is far from the truth! How can I make such a claim, you ask?

The Scripture says in Galatians 3:9, "So then, they that are of faith, the same are the children of Abraham." That means that the moment you accepted Christ as your Savior and your Lord, you were supernaturally grafted into Abraham's family and the body of Christ and you now have a long history of believers as your spiritual heritage!

The Birthright and The Blessing

Have you ever noticed that at the end of their lives, the great patriarchs of the Old Testament would call the family together and they would pass along (impart) the birthright or the blessing to the eldest male child before dying? We see it clearly illustrated in the well-known story of the death of Isaac, Abraham's son. You will remember that Isaac had twin sons, Esau and Jacob. Isaac was very fond of Esau and his wife, Rebekah, was very fond of Jacob. Just prior to their father's death, Jacob deceived Esau into giving him the birthright when Esau was in a weakened state after returning from hunting. Why did Jacob want the birthright or blessing? The birthright meant that you were the one who received not only the majority of the wealth and material assets of the father, but also the headship of the family, both spiritually and practically. You received full authority to lead the family and make decisions about their future. It was an impartation from father to son, which meant all that had been the father's was now the son's. It was the continuation of the blessing of Abraham from generation to generation. Pay attention to how it was transferred!

When Isaac knew he was about to die, he called Esau and said, "Go hunt and prepare me a feast of venison that I may eat, that my soul may bless you before I die" (Gen. 27:2).

When Rebekah (Isaac's wife) heard this, she called Jacob to come while Esau was out hunting, and they plotted to deceive Isaac whose eyes had grown dim and could no longer see properly. Esau was a hairy man so

Rebekah knew that Isaac would undoubtedly touch his arm or lay hands on him and speak the blessing out of his mouth to impart or transfer the birthright or blessing to him, his sons and the generations that followed him. Even in the New Testament, we see the power of laying hands on someone, which can transfer the anointing and bring health and healing. "They shall lay hands on the sick and they shall recover" (Mark 16:18). So you see that the transfer of the blessing was transferred in two ways: by the laying on of hands and by speaking it.

The Power of Words

What are we speaking over our children? By the words that come out of our mouths, we can either bless or curse our children. Have you ever been in a supermarket or someone's house and heard a mother or father in a moment of anger saying something like, "You'll never amount to anything" or "You are a lazy, no good so and so." That parent, whether unwittingly or deliberating, is pronouncing a curse on their child because words are powerful and lodge deeply into the young mind and heart of a child.

Speak The Blessing

Godly parents recognize that they have the power to speak the blessing over their children ... the word of the Lord, words of affirmation and praise ... and their children will grow to be blessed with a God-given confidence in who they were created to be, becoming mature, successful and prosperous adults. My wife, Mindy, and I weren't perfect parents, but one thing we determined to do when raising our son, Daniel James, was to bless him by speaking the Word over him and to him in our conversations and times of learning and living. We didn't give him false praise, but when the occasion warranted positive words of praise, we were quick to give them.

Since the time Daniel was born, my ministry has involved traveling and sometimes being away for extended periods of time. For that reason my wife and I determined that one of us would always be home so that he had a constant presence of godly parenting in his life. I have to compliment my wife, Mindy, for doing an excellent job with sowing faith seeds into Daniel's young life when I was away, even home schooling him for several years which gave her the opportunity to additionally speak godly values into him.

Be Vigilant

With the progressive left mindset, and anti-Christian persuasion happening in many schools these days, Christian parents need to prayerfully consider who is speaking into their young children's impressionable spirits and what they are speaking! This is often very subtle and only with the discernment of the Holy Spirit can these humanistic and progressive persuasions be unmasked! You may need to come to the decision like we did that we needed to for at least a few developmental years, shield our son from ungodly and a down right antagonistic system of thought to what we believe as Christians. When I was home, I was very much involved in his upbringing and I prayed often to the Lord that the bond that my son and I had would continue into adulthood. The Lord heard my prayer and we love each other deeply and still have a close relationship with each other.

We also prayed for his future wife long before he was old enough to even be thinking about getting married. We asked the Lord to bring him a wife that loves the Lord and would help him to continue to be faithful in his walk with the Lord and to become all that God intended for him to be in his life.

Daniel has grown up to be a wonderful young man with a gentle and kind spirit with wisdom beyond his years. He loves the Lord and has been a blessing from the day he was born ... a son that we have always been very proud of! By the way, the Lord heard our prayers and brought his beautiful and lovely wife, Linsey into the family in June of 2013.

As the priest of your family, I encourage you to lay hands on your children at times to impart your faith to them and speak the blessing over them in prayer, believing that as the patriarchs did centuries ago, a heavenly transfer and blessing will be imparted. When you pray for your children, about their future, about their future wives, pray out loud, or speak the blessing over them and watch the Lord fulfill His divine plans for their lives. Pray the Word when you pray; the Word is powerful, alive and God-breathed.

"God of Abraham, Isaac and Jacob" — Our Family Tree

Did you ever notice that when the patriarchs of the Old Testament cried out to God in prayer, they would begin their prayers by saying, "Oh God, of Abraham, Isaac and Jacob?" Why did they invoke the memory of their ancestors in faith when approaching Jehovah God?

I believe that they were saying to God in reverence, "I have history with You!" "I come from a long line of faith and believers!" "As You were faithful to them and heard their cries for help and deliverance, hear mine also, Lord!" "As You demonstrated Your power in their lives and blessed them, bless me also, I pray!" I don't believe that it upset the Lord God to hear them pray this way and in fact, I believe He likes it when we remind Him of history of faith and trust in Him and brings Him pleasure and He will respond accordingly.

We should do the same and follow their example. Remind the Lord that we come from a long line of believers who have trusted and believed in His Word and that we are the benefactors of that faith and blessing and are believing for the same supernatural favor, intervention and blessing that He blessed our ancestors with! The Bible also states, "The effectual, fervent prayer of a righteous man [or woman] avails much" (James 5:16). I am grateful for the prayers of my godly grandparents and parents on my behalf and I believe that the Lord is honoring those prayers even today and fulfilling them even now in my life, long after they have gone to be with Jesus. Even greater still, Jesus, Himself, according to the Word of God, is ever-interceding (praying) for you and me and bringing us before the throne of the Father. He is the Beloved of His Father and we are "accepted in the beloved" (Eph. 1:6). You and I are sons and daughters of the Most High God and have been adopted into a family of faith … a heritage that stems back centuries long.

God's Hall of Faith — Our Family Tree Continued

Those who love sports are very familiar with "The Hall of Fame" in which those who have excelled in sports of baseball and other sports, and have achieved above average stats are often inducted into. The Bible also has a unique group of distinguished men and women who achieved far more than any earthly sports star ever did and were remembered in God's "Hall of Faith," as I call it, for their trust in Him and the mighty works that they did in His Name. These are yours and my ancestors in the faith! You will find it in the book of Hebrews in the Bible, chapter eleven. In fact, after giving a Biblical definition of what faith is in verse one, "The substance of things hoped for, the evidence of things not seen" as our Father Abraham possessed, the writer goes on to say, "For by it the elders [those who have been our spiritual forefathers] obtained a good report" (Heb. 11:2).

If you read on in Hebrews 11, you will see that he begins to list those who "by faith" did amazing, impossible things in the natural and were not only remembered by God but commended for their faith.

"By faith Abel offered unto God a more excellent sacrifice than Cain" (vs. 4)

"By faith Enoch was translated [to heaven] that he should not see death" (vs. 5)

"By faith Noah....prepared an ark to the saving of his house (vs 7)

"By faith Abraham when he was tried, offered up Isaac ...(vs 17)

And on and on it goes to talk about many more like Isaac, Jacob, Joseph and their heirs, all of whom passed their faith from one generation to the next and believed the God of their fathers to do exploits for them as He did for their fathers.

So you see why I said at the beginning of the chapter, that even if you weren't born naturally into a Christian family and came to Christ as an adult, you are as much a part of a long heritage of Godly men and women as I am, and you possess by the breath of God the same ability to believe God for supernatural things to happen in your life!

Let their testimony of God's faithfulness encourage your heart to believe God as they did and you will prove Him to be your heavenly Father and receive your birthright through Christ, His Son.

I hope that after reading this chapter you have become persuaded of your rich and long inheritance of faith as a believer … a faith and inheritance that reaches back hundreds of years and offers countless testimonials of God's miraculous intervention, abundant grace and favor, eternal promises of righteous, peace, joy and God's unending love for you! All that is necessary is for you to believe what He has promised, act in faith on those promises, and expect the blessing of Abraham, your rightful inheritance through Christ, to unleash the same supernatural demonstration of that power in your life on a daily basis. I challenge you to pray bold prayers and believe for the "exceeding, abundantly above all that you can ask or think" blessing of the Lord. I assure you, He will honor His Word and you will soon see amazing thins happen as a result of it. You will see God do miracles and supernatural things!

The Blessing of Faith to Believe for the Impossible

Let's make no mistake about it! What God promised to Abraham was …impossible … at least in the natural realm! Having a child when both you and your wife are well beyond child baring years? Seems a little crazy to believe, even to us centuries later. However, the Bible says, "For with God nothing will be impossible" (Luke 1:37 NKJV). Notice that this verse says, "with God." That means that when we bring God into our impossible situation, nothing will be impossible with His intervention. God is not limited to the parameters that we are in this earthly world. His power and ability are beyond our human comprehension which is why it takes faith to believe outside our finite thinking in a God whose greatness and power is unfathomable. God gave us His written Word replete with miraculous accounts to help us imagine and believe as countless others did for breakthrough and miracles!

The Magnitude of Our Inheritance

One of my most favorite portions of scripture for many years has been Romans 4:20 and 21, which says, "He [speaking of Abraham] staggered not at the promise of God through unbelief but was strong in faith giving glory to God. That what He (the Lord) had promised, He was able also to perform."

Oh, that you and I could realize that part of our inheritance as the children of Abraham is that very same kind of faith that our Father Abraham received when God visited his life; faith that does not stagger or waver in unbelief. Faith that though it has nothing tangible to go on, sees nothing visible or yet manifested in the earthly life, simply trusts that if God said it, it will be so!

I believe that this is a vital part of "the blessing of Abraham." It is part of the legacy that has been transferred to us through Jesus' death and resurrection (Gal. 3:13-14). If we can only realize what is ours in Christ, we will see it work miraculously in our every day lives. This kind of faith is not conjured up or worked up by repeating a scripture verse over and over; it's not mind over matter or in any way produced by the flesh or even our human intellect. It is imparted to us by the Holy Spirit and just as it was quickening to Abram and Sarai's bodies who were dead reproductively, it still brings healing and wholeness today. Hallelujah!

The Holy Spirit makes the Word of God and the promises of God given in the Word real to our hearts and when that happens, it becomes alive in us and sparks faith to believe. "Faith comes by hearing, and hearing by the Word of God" (Rom. 10:17). I am convinced that true faith, the kind that brings about miracles and makes impossible things happen, is a result of the Spirit of Grace breathing it into one's spirit, thereby lifting that person out of the realm of unbelief and into the realm where the miraculous operates.

Don't Doubt God's Promises

If ever a man had reason to question God's promise to him, it was Abraham. God had promised him a son, but as Abraham got closer and closer to 100 years of age, he could very easily have doubted God's promise to him. But he didn't. Abraham never doubted or questioned God's promise to him; he was strong in his faith, never doubting that God would fulfill His promise to him.

Near the beginning of this chapter I shared a passage from Romans 4 that has been one of my favorite portions of scripture for many years. It's so powerful that I want to include it again ... this time from the Amplified version, which clearly points out the victory of Abraham's faith and trust in God: "He did not weaken in faith when he considered the [utter] impotence of his own body, which was as good as dead because he was about a hundred years old, or [when he considered] the barrenness of Sarah's [deadened] womb. No unbelief or distrust made him waver [doubtingly question] concerning the promise of God, but he grew strong and was empowered by faith as he gave praise and glory to God, fully satisfied and assured that God was able and mighty to keep His word and to do what He had promised" (Rom. 4:19-21, AMP).

Trusting The Word of the Lord

In 2011 my wife and I had an opportunity to trust God for something that seemed impossible in the natural. One day while I have having my quiet time with the Lord, I heard these words in my spirit: "Believe Me for a mortgage-free house." At that time, my wife, Mindy, and I were still living in Southern California and although we loved the area and were close to family and friends, things had changed and we were in a new season, making it difficult to keep up with the large mortgage payments plus property taxes on what had been our lovely home since moving from Florida in July of 1999. We had stepped out by faith into a new season, and no longer had a regular salary to depend on; we were (and still are) completely dependent on the Lord to provide through the love offerings and honorariums from preaching in churches as well as donations from those that support our ministry.

For almost three years the Lord had been amazingly faithful to supply and provide for our needs since stepping out into our new season of ministry in January of 2010, but when there were gaps in my schedule, it made it hard to meet the monthly budget and pay the mortgage payment. Southern California is beautiful but it is also one of the most expensive real estate markets in the country so our mortgage at that time was over $400,000 still, with a mortgage payment of approximately $2,000.00 per month. On top of that, we had a rental property with a mortgage of over $200,000, which we had purchased in those years when we had more consistent income and it seemed a wise investment. All together, the mortgages on the two properties totaled over $600,000.

I remembered years ago, when a member of the church in Orlando had felt led of the Lord to pay off Pastor Benny and Suzanne's house mortgage and what a huge blessing and relief it was to them and an answer to a word of faith that the Lord had given him for a mortgage-free home. I believed that God could do it because I have always known and believed the Word that says, "Nothing is impossible with God." Yet, somehow, the concept of it ever happening to me was not something I could get hold of in my spirit or even think that it could ever happen for us.

The Faith Challenge

Thoughts like this filled my mind and challenged my faith: "That only happens to the Mega Ministers, not to guys like me — Jim Cernero."

So now the Lord is speaking to my spirit saying, "Why don't you believe me for a mortgage-free home?" At that moment, a Word of Faith was dropped into my spirit and everything in me embraced it and believed now that if God could do it for them, He could certainly make it happen for us. I quickly got out my journal, as I always do when I believe the Lord is speaking to me or if He's revealing something to me while reading His Word, and wrote down a faith declaration: "today, Lord, I am believing You for a mortgage-free home so that I can travel and minister freely, unencumbered by a heavy monthly mortgage payment obligation." I remember that I spoke it out of my mouth also. I believe that when God gives you a Word of faith, it is not only important to write it down but also to speak it out of your mouth. Why? I believe that both writing it down and speaking it aloud sets things in motion in the Spirit realm. The Word is clear … "You shall have whatsoever you say" (Mk. 11:22-24).

For several weeks I spoke it out audibly in my times of prayer and devotions but as time went on, to be honest, I forgot about it. Now, it's the fall of 2011 and one day both Mindy and I mutually said to each other, "It's time for us to move … to Texas." Texas? I had never dreamed I would ever live in the state of Texas and also to be honest, didn't really want to. Too hot, I thought. Too flat, and so on. But, God has a way of bringing us around to what's best for us! He will situate us for favor if we will just be open to His voice, listen, and obey it. At the time our son, Daniel was attending Baylor University in Waco, Texas, had fallen in love with a "Texan" by the name of Linsey, and it seemed to us pretty definitely that his/their life, once they married, would be in Texas. Since Daniel is our only child, we didn't want to be thousands of miles away from him, his soon-to-be wife, and our future grandchildren.

Faith and Favor

We put our home in California up for sale and within two months it had sold. When we moved to California in 1999, it was a "buyer's market" but shortly afterwards, the boom of the early 2000s came and our house quickly jumped up in value several hundred thousand dollars. Favor! When the Spirit of the Lord is on your life, He will breathe favor into every aspect of your life … including your finances!

We sold our home at a reasonable profit, packed up everything (what a job after 12 years) and drove to Texas. For the first four months, we decided to rent a small (I repeat SMALL!) apartment in Austin, Texas while looking for a house and finding the right neighborhood, etc. Needless to say, after the four months, we were MORE than ready to get out of that tiny apartment! So was Jackson, our cute Cavalier King Charles dog!

Sorry! You Don't Qualify!

We finally found a lovely house in a golf community (I'm not a golfer by any means but we liked the neighborhood) and began to make plans for the purchase. We didn't have enough money from our California house to pay cash and buy it outright, so I began the process of applying for a loan/mortgage for the balance needed to purchase the home. Wouldn't you know, we got turned down! For the first time in our married lives, after having above average credit and always being able to get the financing for our homes, we are suddenly in the awkward position of being told, "Sorry … you don't qualify!"

At first we were discouraged but then all of a suddenly, I heard in my spirit, "Weren't you believing Me for a mortgage-free home?" My heart leaped and I said out loud, "Yes, Lord, I was." I can't explain it but suddenly faith rose up in my heart to believe once again for that mortgage-free home that the Lord had spoken to me about previously. I went and found my journal where I had written it down months before and faith began to build again for it. I believe that when the Blessing of Abraham is on your life, God quickens or makes alive your faith for the impossible.

I began to not only pray about it but I also began to speak it out of my mouth and confess, "We will have a mortgage-free home." Now, mind you, I was thinking that God would speak to some financially blessed person who could just write me a check as I had seen happen to others, but God sometimes will work in ways we can't even imagine and give us a "creative thought" or a "God idea" as I call it to bring about His promise. Deuteronomy 8:18 says, "But thou shalt remember the Lord thy God; for it is He that giveth thee power to get wealth…" In other words, He will give you an idea, or a promotion or an ability to prosper through a business deal, invention or sales transaction or the like which will then bring wealth and financial blessing.

God is my witness, as all this was going through my mind and spirit, I got what I believe was a God idea. I remembered that I had a retirement account or 403-b as it's called. I had never thought of borrowing from it and quite frankly, didn't even know there was a provision in the contract that allows for a one time loan that you then pay it off (or pay yourself back) in monthly installments. I called the provider and sure enough, they said I qualified for the loan and provided me with the necessary application form to fill out. Within a matter of no more than two weeks, we had the balance of the funds needed to purchase the home and we were ecstatic about moving out of that crowded little apartment and into a lovely home that was even larger and newer than our home in California ... and it was mortgage-free! Of course, I had to pay back the loan to the retirement account but it was paying myself or us back and not some bank or holder of our mortgage. So, in a sense, I took a loan from myself and we were able to pay cash for the home.

God's Promise Fulfilled

I will never forget the conversation I had with the property insurance person. She said, "Now Reverend Cernero, how will you be financing the home?" With a smile on my face I said, "We're not! We're buying it outright and paying cash for it." There was a moment of silence on the other end of the phone and then she said, "Well, that's just great!" Needless to say, we were praising the Lord for His glorious answer to the Word of faith that He gave me several years earlier. Footnote, we were able to pay that loan back to our retirement account in a matter of months and we owe $0 on the house! Isn't the Lord amazing?

And as an added blessing, when we purchased our home in Texas, it was a buyer's market again and the house we are now living in was a "short sale" which we purchased for $45,000 less than it was valued at! The house has since appreciated over $100K since we moved in just three short years ago! Praise The Lord!

Dare To Trust God For The Impossible

Why am I telling you this, dear reader? Not to brag but to encourage your heart to believe for faith to trust

God for what may seem to you an impossibility with no way of coming about. I believe that this happened as a direct result of the Spirit of the Lord breathing faith into my heart to believe for a miracle, and once my heart got ahold of that promise, it was just a matter of time before God would fulfill it miraculously.

He wants to do the same for you! What are you believing for? Is it a healing for your body? A reconciliation of a relationship that has gone wrong? A financial miracle? Whatever it is, know this! When God's Holy Spirit breathes the Blessing of Abraham on your heart and life, it can bring about miraculous things!

I want to remind you, I received that word of faith when I was in a time of prayer and fellowship with the Lord. It's there that He breathes on us, quickens us and makes alive His promises and Word to us. He's no respecter of persons; if He did it for me, He can do it for you. But don't just take my word for it or what happened to us; look in the Word of God and you will see many more amazing examples of those who trusted God to do something miraculous and their faith brought about almost incredible exploits and miraculous happenings.

I shared with you the story of Zerubbabel in Chapter Three, The Blessing of Grace, and how that when the Word of the Lord spoken by the Prophet Zechariah was received and acted upon, it brought about what had previously been impossible. Zerubbabel by the power of the Holy Spirit was able to accomplish the task of rebuilding the city acting on the Word of the Lord which said, "Not by might, nor by power, but by My Spirit, says the Lord of Hosts."

It is interesting to note that another translation of this well-known verse puts it this way: "Not by might, nor by power but by the breath of Almighty God!" I love this version because it reminds us that the same power that breathed into Abraham and Sarah, that enabled Zerubbabel to bring about the impossible, is ours today as part of the blessing!

It is important for us to realize that as part of the blessing that we have received as children of Abraham and as believers in Christ Jesus, we have access to supernatural grace and power to make the impossible, possible!

When I depart for a ministry trip, I always ask the Lord that He will work with me as He did with the apostles of the early church and do the impossible as He did through them. I do this because of what Mark 16:20 says. "And they went forth, and preached everywhere, the Lord working with them, and confirming the Word with signs following. Amen." I am always amazed at how He answers this prayer and does exactly that.

For example, early in 2013 I traveled to the country of Brazil and ministered at several churches. I love going to Brazil because it seems there is a hunger in many of the churches for the fire of God and for the demonstration of God's supernatural power. How I pray that that will be the case more so in our churches here in America once again!

Miracles Before My Eyes

In one of the services, I felt led to step off the platform and go out among the people who were believing

God for their healing. Each time I do that in a service, I ask the Holy Spirit to lead me. I ask that He will deposit faith in the hearts of those needing a miracle for the impossible to happen and ask that He would increase my faith to believe with them as well! I approached a woman who was legally blind and could only see shadows. I asked her through the interpreter what she was believing God for. She replied that she wanted her sight restored. As I always do, I asked, "Do you believe that God is able to restore your eyesight and give you a miracle?" She said, "Si, si!" (yes, yes!) I laid hands on her as the Word tells us to do and spoke healing, declaring, "By His stripes you are healed." Instantly and right before my eyes, she screamed and exclaimed in Portuguese, the language of the Brazilians, "I can see, I can see!" We rejoiced with her and praised the Lord for "working with us" and bringing about this wonderful healing! This, my friend, is an example of what I am trying to express in this chapter. Part of our inheritance as believers and as recipients of the blessing of Abraham is the same miracle working power to bring about what in the natural would be impossible ... like this precious woman's eyesight being restored. It was when her faith came into agreement with the Word of God that she received her miracle.

A man also later testified in that very same service that as I walked by him, his back was instantly healed! PTL! He had been sitting there throughout the service in agony, hardly able to endure it and in a moment, the Spirit of the Lord touched him and healed his back. He later said when giving testimony of his healing, that when I simply walked by him seated in the front row, he was healed at the very moment. I quickly said to him, "It was Jesus who walked by you and who healed you; I am just the instrument through which He worked in that moment."

Witnessing a dramatic healing like this first hand, right before your eyes, does something to your own faith and causes you to realize the power we have in the mighty name of Jesus. I believe the Lord wants to heal His people and meet their needs but sadly, we have been conditioned to believe that this sort of miracle don't happen in our day. Jesus hasn't changed; His power is still the same as it was over 2,000 years ago when He walked the earth. The miracles He performed were a direct fulfillment of Isaiah's prophecy in Isaiah 35:5: "The eyes of the blind shall be opened…" This is what happens when the Spirit of the Lord breathes into your heart. He causes your faith to become stronger and you step out and minister to those in need around you. By the way, this is not only relegated to those who are called to full-time ministry. "They shall lay hands on the sick and they shall recover" was not intended for an exclusive group of healing evangelists. The "they" are you and me … all of us who are part of the body of Christ. We are called to ministry in one way or another, and if we just ask the Lord to work with us, we will see miracles and the power of God in demonstration more often!

By the way, I believe that we should call on the Holy Spirit's aid in the little matters or what may seem too insignificant to bring before the Lord as well as the major issues where we need His intervention. He told us to "cast all our care on Him" and all means all. Let me share an example of what may seem like a small thing but I assure you, to me, it wasn't.

The Lost Contact Lens

Like many individuals, I wear contact lenses. One morning while attempting to put my left contact lens in, I somehow lost it. For those of you who are lens wearers, you know that this does not make for the beginning of a good day! After searching for over an hour and almost resigning myself to the fact that my missing contact lens had gone into that "infamous black hole into which a lens goes," I decided to ask the Holy Spirit to help me find it. I prayed a simple little prayer such as this: "Holy Spirit, you know I need to see clearly to do what is required of me today; please help me find this contact lens." Just after praying this prayer, I decided to go back and take one more look around for it.

As I went back to the bathroom and began looking for the missing contact lens, I kept asking the Holy Spirit to help me find it. Standing right where I had stood before during my unsuccessful search, I slowly looked one more time … and there, right next to the tissue box (on the side that was facing away from me) I discovered my lost contact lens! It had been there the entire time! I started thanking the Lord because nothing is too small or too large for God. As the Word of God declares, "WITH God, nothing will be impossible" (Luke 1:37, NKJV). All we have to do is ask!

It is interesting to note that one of the first references to healing is found all the way back in Genesis 20:17. Abraham prays for God to heal the barrenness of King

Abimlelech's wives and they soon after bore children to him. Barrenness, or not being able to have children, is an emotionally painful condition and my wife, Mindy, and I know that from personal experience.

Early on in our marriage, my wife, Mindy and I desired greatly to have a child. After three years of marriage, still no baby. After a physical exam, it was discovered that she had endometriosis, a condition in which dead cell tissue builds up and prevents pregnancy. She had to have a laparoscopy to remove the dead cells, etc., but still no success in getting pregnant. It was an emotional roller coaster for us, but especially for Mindy.

If memory serves me correctly, it was several months later in November of 1987 that we received the call to come to be the Minister of Music/Worship Leader for Orlando Christian Center in Orlando, Florida where Pastor Benny Hinn was pastor and where his ministry was based at the time. Shortly after joining the staff, I woke up at 2:30 a.m. and although I didn't hear an audible voice, I heard the Lord speak these words of faith to my spirit which said, "You're going to have a son." I remember tears coming down my face, and as I laid there, I was not sure whether or not to wake Mindy because of all that she had been through in the past. I had been a bachelor for ten years in ministry before meeting and marrying my beautiful wife, Mindy, and one of the deepest desires of my heart was to have a child; hearing those words was overwhelming to say the least! I also wept tears of gratitude because, as I shared in the chapter on the Blessing of Peace, one of the things the devil had told me several years before when I went through that horrible experience in Bible College was, "You'll never be a father." Now the Lord was proving His faithfulness to me and giving us our heart's desire for a child. The devil is truly a liar! The very next day, I shared this amazing experience with my wife and we rejoiced together believing that soon, the word of the Lord would come true for us. Without me knowing it, later that day, Mindy took a pregnancy test and it came out positive.

The Joy of Answered Prayer

Sitting at my desk working in my office a few hours later, one of the administrative assistants came to my office door with balloons from Mindy which said, "Rock-a-bye-Baby" on them which, of course, was to let me know I was going to a Dad and we were going to be parents ... a miracle from the Lord! I can't begin to tell you the joy that I experienced in that moment and that Mindy and I shared, knowing that the Lord, who knows the desire of our hearts, had heard our prayer and answered and the long season of barrenness was coming to an end.

On September 14, 1988, Daniel James Cernero was born and since that day, he has brought us nothing but joy and blessing. He's now 26 years old and is married to a beautiful girl named Linsey.

These are just a few of the many miracles that have happened in not only my personal life but also that I have witnessed over many years of ministry. I pray that they have encouraged you and inspired you to ask the Holy Spirit to give you a Word of faith for your miracle. May this testimonies of God's faithfulness help you come to the awareness that part of your inheritance from Father Abraham is the same ability to believe the promises of God, and the same faith to see divine intervention and supernatural happenings take place in what has seemed impossible up until now.

When I was growing up in church, we used to sing an old chorus that I'd like to close this chapter with. Simple words, but if we can just believe it, we will see the impossible become possible in our every day lives.

"Got any rivers, you think are un-crossable?
Got any mountains, you can't tunnel through?
God specializes in things thought impossible!
And He can do what no other power can do!"
— words and music by Oscar C. Eliason

Simple lyrics but yet they challenge us to step out of our comfort zone and believe God!

A chorus entitled "Healer" by Hillsong says:

"Nothing is impossible for You,
Nothing is impossible!
Nothing is impossible for You,
You hold my world in Your hands!"
— written by Michael Guglielmucci

Whether you're familiar with the first or second song or neither of them, the truth is that nothing is impossible when the blessing of Abraham, the promise of the Spirit, is added to the equation!

The Apostle Paul puts it this way in Ephesians 1:18, "The eyes of your understanding being enlightened;

that you may know what is the hope of His calling, what are the riches of His glory of His inheritance in the saints." One of the reasons that many are lacking in areas of their life, whether it be in healing for their body or financial provision or wisdom in how to deal with a trying situation, is because they need a bigger or larger revelation of the Lord, the One Who is able to "supply all your need according to His riches in glory" (Phil. 4:19). How we see Him, effects what we receive from Him and the measure of His riches in glory we experience.

As a final word in this chapter, I challenge you to spend time in God's presence and let the Spirit of the Lord breathe new life to your vision; grace for healing for your body; faith to believe for the impossible … the ability to receive what's rightfully yours as a child of Abraham and as a believer in Christ Jesus!

CHAPTER NINE

The Blessing of Abundance

From even a very casual reading of the book of Genesis, it becomes clearly obvious that one of the results of God's presence in not only Abraham's life but in his descendants' lives even as far removed as Joseph, caused them to become very blessed men and women. Definitely part of the blessing of Abraham was financial wealth and material substance.

Wealth Transfer Number 1

Several wealth transfers took place throughout the course of their lives from which they became men of wealth, substance, land holdings and possessions that calculated in today's money, would rival some of the millionaires and billionaires of our day, the first being recorded in Genesis 12 when due to a famine, Abram travels to Egypt. Sarah, Abram's wife, was a beautiful woman and he feared that the Pharaoh of Egypt might kill him and keep her as his wife so he lied to him and told him that she was his sister. The Pharaoh was quite taken with Sarah his wife and gave him sheep, oxen, servants and camels in hopes of making her his wife. After Pharaoh discovered that Abram had lied to him, he became very angry with Abram and sent them away. However, when Abram left, he left with all the wealth given to him by Pharaoh. This, to my knowledge, is the first wealth transfer recorded in the Bible. As you continue reading, this continued throughout Abram's life until he became a very wealthy man by the time he died.

These transfers continued in his son, Isaac's life and unto his son, Jacob and his even down to his son, Joseph and beyond. They are still happening today with the Jewish people because the covenant God made with Abraham in which He (God) said to him, "And I will make my covenant between me and thee, and will multiply thee exceedingly" (Gen. 17:2) is an everlasting covenant.

Have you ever noticed that some of the richest people on earth, some of the most successful businessmen, doctors, lawyers, scientists and so forth, are Jewish? Why do you think that's the case? It's because of this covenant God made to Abraham and his descendants. Down through the generations of time has passed such favor that it is inexplicable with all the attempts to destroy them as a people and can only be attributed to the fact that they are God's chosen people and His favor and blessing has remained on them, despite the fact that many have rejected Him still and don't realize the source of their blessing.

Wealth Transfer Number Two

Isaac receives the wealth of Abimelech as recorded in Genesis 26:10 when he did the same thing as his father, Abraham did and lied about his wife Rebekah being his sister because she too was "easy on the eyes" as we might say today and was afraid that Abimelech, King of the Philistines would put him to death in order to have Rebekah as his wife. Isaac became a very wealthy man also because of this deal he made with Abimelech and verse 13 says, "The man began to prosper, and continued prospering until he became very prosperous." As happened with his father Abraham, he was kicked out when the King looked out his window and noticed that their relationship was more than just that of brother and sister! But not before obtaining great wealth, however!

Wealth Transfer Number Three

Jacob, Isaac's son, goes to stay with his Uncle Laban to escape his brother Esau's wrath because of deceiving their father, Isaac and receiving the birthright (the blessing). While there he falls in love with Laban's daughter, Rachel and agrees to work seven years for her. His deceit catches up with him, though, and when it comes time for him to be given Rachel as his wife, his Uncle Laban tricks him and gives him his not so pretty daughter, Leah instead! In order to be given Rachel, the love of his heart, he is made to work another seven years. All in all, he winds up staying 21 years there and while doing so, becomes a very rich man (Gen. 31:6).

Wealth Transfer Number Four

Joseph, Jacob's son, goes from being rejected by his brothers and sold into slavery to eventually becoming second in command to only Pharaoh in Egypt and acquires vast wealth in the process. Joseph, who also is a type of Christ in the Bible in that he was the beloved son of Jacob, his father because he was born by Rachel, the wife he loved greatly, was rejected by his brothers, as Christ "came onto His own and His own received him not." He is sold as a slave and winds up in prison due to a false accusation. But the Word of God says a very profound thing about Joseph and that one thing caused his eventual triumph and brought him great blessing. Genesis 31:29 says, "But the Lord was *with* Joseph, and showed him mercy, and gave him favor in the sight of the keeper of the prison." When the Lord is *with* you, He will line up favor and blessing (abundance) for you as He did for Joseph. God took him from a prison to a palace. Years later during another famine in Israel, when his brothers hear there is food in Egypt and travel down to get some food, they are providentially brought face to face with their own brother, Joseph, whom they had treated so terribly years before. Once it is revealed that this man who has great power and authority in all of Egypt is none other than their little brother, Joseph, they are very afraid of what he might do to them because of their unjust treatment of him years earlier. But Joseph utters these famous words from Genesis 50:20 to them and lovingly redeems the circumstance and turns it together to be the salvation of Israel: "You meant it for evil, but God meant it for good." He brings the entire family, including his beloved father, Jacob, to stay with him in Egypt to escape the famine (season of lack) and they too, become recipients of Joseph's wealth transfer. Are you starting to see a pattern here?

Wealth Transfer Number Five

Joseph and his children, his brothers and their families, and their descendants stay in Egypt for many years until things become very rough for them under the rule of Pharaoh who did not have kindness toward them as did his predecessors. The Israelites literally become slaves, building the ancient pyramids and were greatly oppressed, crying to be set free. God raises up a deliverer by the name of Moses. Moses, although a Jew by birth, had been raised by Pharaoh's daughter when Pharaoh had ordered that all the first born infants of the Jewish children be killed. To spare her son's life, Moses' mother puts him in a basket and sends him down the Nile River. She sends his sister, Miriam, to watch him and in the end, when discovered by Pharaoh's daughter, she (Moses' sister) tells her she knows of one who can be a proper Jewish nurse maid to the child, their own mother. Moses' mother is brought to help raise him right there in the courts of Pharaoh.

After many years, God ordains for Moses to be the one to help bring about the deliverance of His people and Moses goes to Pharaoh and says, "Let my people go." Pharaoh's heart becomes hardened but after a series of horrible plagues, the last being the death of all the first born in Egypt, he agrees to let Moses and the camp of Israel leave. However, just before they leave, while all of Egypt was grieving over the loss of their first born children, the Israelites borrowed jewels of silver, jewels of gold and clothing. Exodus 12:36 states, "And the Lord gave the people [the Israelites] favor in the sight of the Egyptians, so that they lent unto them such things as they required. And they spoiled [left them bankrupt] the Egyptians." In their sorrow and grief, they were so anxious to get rid of the children of Israel who in their eyes had brought upon them this terrible loss, that they willingly gave up their possessions and basically said, "Take what you want … just leave, go on, get out of here!" When the children of Israel finally leave Egypt, they leave with great wealth and substance. God took them from extreme poverty to prosperity.

Wealth Transfer Number Six

Solomon receives the wealth of the then known world. If you read 1 Kings 9 and 10, it becomes clear that as a result of the favor of God on King Solomon, he received the wealth of many kings and queens, including the Queen of Sheba, who brought him gold, spices (which in those days were very valuable), precious stones and indescribable wealth. So great was his wealth that the Scripture says in 1 Kings 10:23: "So King Solomon exceeded all the Kings of the earth for riches and wisdom." He became famous for it and to this day we refer to him when speaking of financial blessing.

Wealth Transfer Number Seven

I believe there is one last wealth transfer that the Bible mentions. Would you like to know who it is? I believe, the answer is … you! The seventh wealth transfer is to you and me who are as much the children of Abraham as his children by blood and therefore are inheritor's of the blessing of Abraham. You might say, how can you make such a statement? Let me give you several reasons why I believe that next in line for financial blessing are the righteous … those that belong to Christ's body and are part of the family of faith, the children of Abraham.

1. The covenant God made with Abraham in which he would be the "father of nations" and "in him would all of the nations of the earth be blessed" was and is an eternal covenant. It will never end! Centuries later, the descendants of Abraham, both by blood and ethnicity and those who are children by spiritual adoption through faith in Christ, (Gal. 3:9) are still favored and are the rightful inheritors of that blessing. Remember, part of the blessing that was on Abraham, then his son, Isaac and Isaac's son Jacob and Jacob's son, Joseph and so on was abundance and financial blessing.

2. God deals with us, the church, in a similar manner as He did with the Israelites, His chosen people. When He brought them out of Egypt, not only did they leave with the wealth of Egypt (which in the Bible is a type of the world and worldly system) but the Word says "there was not one feeble among them" (Ps. 105:37). He brought them out in physical health and strength also. The blessing of abundance affects all aspects of our lives, not just financially, but includes our health, mental and emotional welfare, and total well-being (The Shalom blessing) for every facet of our beings.

3. Deuteronomy 28 outlines the many benefits and blessings of obeying the law of God. In Christ, Who is the fulfillment of the law and our righteousness (2 Cor. 5:21) we qualify for those same blessings mentioned in Deuteronomy 28 such as: blessing that "overtakes you"

(vs 2) / being "blessed in the city and in the field" (vs 3) / "the fruit of your body" (your children) being blessed (vs 4) / "the fruit of your ground, cattle, sheep" (vs. 4) (translates today to our business or means of income) / "blessed shall be your basket and your store" (vs 5) (what you have in your wallet and what you have in your bank account) / "blessed when you come in and when you go out" (vs 6) (blessed everywhere you are) and it goes on and on as you keep reading chapter 28 of Deuteronomy. Now some might say, "Well brother, that's Old Testament; it's not for us today." I believe the Bible (Old and New Testaments) is the inspired (God-breathed) Word of the Living God who changes not. His ways, His heart towards His people, and His Word to them are immutable, a large word that means He does not change! Besides, you may have heard this very true expression: the Old Testament is in the New Testament "revealed" and the New Testament is in the Old Testament "concealed". Many of the things God did and had His chosen people do were foreshadows of His perfect work on the cross which provides abundance for us in every way.

4. The Word of God repeatedly says that He will bless His people, including scriptures like the following:

"A good man leaves an inheritance to his children's children and the wealth of the sinner is laid up for the just" (Prov. 13:22).

"The Lord shall increase you, you and your children more and more" (Ps. 116:14).

"You crown the year with goodness; your paths drip with abundance" (Ps. 65:11). (I will talk more about this amazing verse in just a moment; stay tuned.)

Deuteronomy 28:1-10, which I referred to above.

Job 27:16-17, speaking of the sinner says,"Though he heap up silver as the dust, and prepare clothing as the clay 17 He may prepare it but the just [the righteous] shall put it on and the innocent [the pure in heart] shall divide the silver."

Job 36:11 states, "If they obey and serve Him, they shall spend their days in prosperity, and their years in pleasures."

Proverbs 8:21 says, "That I may cause those that love me, to inherit wealth; that I may fill their treasures."

Matthew 6:33 declares, "But seek first the Kingdom of God and His righteousness, and all these things [including financial blessing] shall be added to you."

Luke 6:38 says, "Give [if you are a believer, you will then be a giver] and it will be given to you: good measure, pressed down, and shaken together, and running over shall men give into your bosom. For with the same measure that you use, it will be measured back to you."

I could go on and on giving you scriptures to back up this truth that it is God's desire and heart to bless His people with abundance financially and in every other way, but I believe you are getting the point!

5. If you look at the life and ministry of Jesus when He was here on earth, it becomes obvious that His pres-

ence brought abundance. Jesus was born into a poor family in extreme poverty. Scripture tells us in Luke 2 that He was delivered in a lowly manger (certainly not where you would expect a King to be born) because there was "no room for Him in the inn" (Luke 2:7). However, His family didn't stay poor for very long! Matthew 2:1 tells us that when Jesus was born in Bethlehem of Judea, "There came wise men from the East to Jerusalem." If you keep reading the account, it says this in verse 11: "And when they were come into the house, they saw the young child with Mary, His mother and fell down, and worshipped Him; and when they had opened their treasures, they presented unto Him gifts; gold, and frankincense and myrrh." His very presence brought wealth and abundance! I believe that if He is living in you and me, His presence will still bring abundance and blessing financially to us also.

Have there been abuses, especially with some Christian TV personalities who have gone to excess and greed in their pursuit of fame and fortune and abused the generous gifts of their viewing audiences? Absolutely! I have seen quite a lot in my many years of ministry and all that I can say is, they will one day have to give an account of how they handled the money and resources that God gave them.

On the other hand, does poverty or lack financially bring glory to God? Does having a poverty mentality and always looking at what you don't have rather than what God has promised us make us more like the Lord? If we believe that we serve the King of Kings, does it bring Him honor when we don't believe for the abundance that He Himself promised us in His Word? I don't believe so.

Do I feel that it is wrong for a Christian to want nice things and to be blessed financially? No, but it comes down to where your heart is! The Bible says, "Where your heart is, so will your treasure be also." If the Lord Jesus is the center of your life and heart, He will make your desires and priorities those of His heart.

Is it wrong for a Christian to drive a nice, late model vehicle or live in a lovely home and have some of the finer things? No, absolutely not … as long as these things do not have them, if you know what I mean.

Why should the Christian and believer in Christ desire to be blessed financially? To spread the gospel of Jesus Christ. You may have heard the expression, "The gospel is free but the delivery of the gospel, at least by means of traveling to preach or participate in evangelist outreaches, television ministry, internet and so on, are not free." It takes money to do all of these things.

Does it not take money to support Christian missionaries, orphanages, various outreaches, charities and such? Of course it does. So why not believe the Word of God and ask Him to bless you like Jabez did in 1 Chronicles 4:10 and expect that God will do for you as He did for Jabez? Jabez said, "Oh, that You would bless me indeed!" (in other words, a lot!) I believe that when you give, He will increase your ability to give and prosper you accordingly. I have proven this over and over in my life, not only by tithing but giving offerings to the Lord's work. I believe that the devil himself has convinced Christians that it's not right to believe for abundance and prosperity in order to thwart the work of the Kingdom and hinder its advancement! If he can keep us under the mindset that poverty is somehow a virtue, then he's won the battle.

As we look at Jesus' later years in ministry, when He showed up on the scene, miracles of provision took place! Examples like the parable of the loaves and fishes (Matt. 14:14-22) where a multitude of 5,000 were fed from five loaves of bread and two fish demonstrate that His very presence brought multiplication of the little lunch that a boy had, so much so that there was even leftovers!

Simon's Great Catch

Another time, when a crowd had gathered around Jesus by the lake of Gennesaret, He noticed two boats, one of them belonging to Simon. Scripture tells us that He entered his boat and began teaching them. While He was speaking, he tells Simon to launch out into the deep and let down his nets for a draught (a large draw of fish). Simon responds and says, "Master, we have toiled all the night and have taken nothing; nevertheless, at Your Word I will let down the net" (Luke 5:4). As a result of his obedience to the Word of the Lord, when he let down the net, a "multitude of fishes" (Luke 5:6) were caught in the nets to the point that the net began to break. They had to call the other boat over for assistance and still there was such a large catch that both boats began to sink! That's abundance! Note that it wasn't until Jesus stepped into the boat that the abundance came. Once again, we see His presence bringing blessing!

Footnote to the this parable: Several years ago, a couple of young boys from a Kibbutz near this very same lake in Israel discovered a boat from the time of Christ that became exposed in the mud when the lake water level was low due to a drought. It was carefully and methodically extracted by archaeologists and has since been preserved in a museum that I have gone to on my visits to the Holy Land. No one knows for sure who the boat belonged to but maybe … just maybe … it was the very same boat that Jesus and the disciples were in and from which this amazing miracle happened!

Once again, I could give example after example of proof that when Jesus is present, miracles of provision, healing and abundance take place. His presence in the life of the believer still does the same today!

I listed Psalm 65:11 earlier when I gave the list of scriptures that speak about blessing, but I'd like to share what I discovered as I studied this verse and pray that it will bless you as it has blessed me.

At the beginning of each new year we often hear many prophetic words about the coming year being a year of abundance, breakthrough, restoration, favor, divine provision and the like. While many of these may be inspired by the Holy Spirit, the fact is by mid year, there seems to be less talk about the actual realization of these words and if we're being honest, many are not experiencing the blessings that were prophesied at the beginning of the year with such passion and conviction.

The 365-Day Blessing of Abundance

Dear reader, I believe the blessing of abundance isn't just a seasonal or occasional thing but rather something that the Lord wants us to experience 365 days a year! Take a look at what the Psalmist David wrote about the subject and keep in mind that David wrote two-thirds of the Psalms in which the content largely declares the goodness and abundance that God promises. Here's what David said to the Lord: "You crown the year with goodness; Your paths drip with abundance" (Ps. 65:11). These words penned by David are saying that everyday, no matter when it falls in the calendar year, is an opportunity to see Your favor, Lord. The word "crown" means to surround you with blessing. In other words, when the Lord's presence is in your life, His glory touches every aspect of your life and brings abundance ... abundance of peace, abundance of joy, abundance of health and healing, abundance to your finances and everything you put your hands to do.

More Than Enough

The word "abundance" that David uses at the end of this verse means what you would expect it to mean: more than enough, plenty and fatness. Whenever you see the word "fatness" used in Scripture, it is most often referring to abundance of being blessed with bounty. The derivation of this word abundance is the Hebrew word "deshen," which means superabundance but it also means ashes. Ashes, you say? Let me explain. When the priests of the Old Testament sacrificed an animal on the altar for a burnt offering, after slaying the animal they would burn it until there was nothing left on the altar but ashes. What is the final state of anything that is burnt? Ashes. When the ashes appeared on the altar it was a sign that the work was finished! The work was done and had been accomplished. Sound familiar? Indeed! They were a symbolic foreshadowing of the perfect, finished work of our Savior, the spotless Lamb of God on Calvary which provides not only for the saving of the soul, but provision for every facet of our lives. When He (Jesus) cried, "It is finished," He forever paid the price for us to be provided abundance in every aspect of our lives! No lack because Jehovah-Jireh, the Lord who provides, is with us. Just as He provided a ram as a substitute for Abraham's son Isaac, so He has provided for and paid the sacrifice for you and me. David was both reflecting back on the sacrifices which he undoubtedly realized spoke of provision and abundance, but was also prophetically speaking of the work of Christ hundreds of years later which speak "ashes" or abundance and no lack to us in every way! PTL! So today, expect "deshen" upon your life 365 days of the year and declare "ashes" when you see an area of lack in your life, and watch the finished work of the cross of Jesus provide for you.

Maybe you've gotten a little discouraged because you have yet to experience this blessing of abundance that I've been telling you is yours in Christ. Remember, DELAYED blessing does not mean DENIED blessing! God is never late! His promise to Abraham may have appeared to be late by natural standards, but in God's timing, it was right on time. Because of their ages Abraham and Sarah had no other option than to trust God to fulfill His promise to them. Hebrews 6:15 says, "And so, after he [Abraham] had patiently endured, he obtained the promise."

Most of us are familiar with the fact that it took many years for God's promise to Abraham to be fulfilled and come to pass. I'm sure that many times over those many years, Abraham struggled with questions like, "When, Lord? When is this going to happen? I'm not exactly a young man, Lord." We all have thoughts like this when the answer that we have been waiting for seems like it's taking forever to come or when we've been holding on to a promise from God's Word and after much time has passed, there is no sign of it coming about nor a manifestation of the promise. With the birth of Isaac came the fulfillment of God's promise to make Abraham the father of many nations. The above referenced verse was included in Hebrews, I believe, to encourage us that if the Lord was true to His Word with our Father, Abraham, so He will be true to His Word to us. We must, like Abraham, "patiently endure" … as hard as that is to do at times … and eventually we will see it come about.

As I wrap up this chapter on the blessing of abundance, I would like to draw your attention to two more passages of scripture that I believe show us that when God's presence, or His glory, is in your life, so there will be abundance.

Haggai 2:7-9 gives a prophecy of what will happen in the world in the end times, but more importantly, what will happen in the church of Jesus Christ. Let's look at it:

"And I will shake all nations, *[just watch the news and you see this is happening]* and the desire of nations *[Jesus]* shall come; and I will fill this house with glory, says the Lord of hosts." (vs.7)

"The silver is mine, and the gold is mine says the Lord of hosts." (vs. 8) It is interesting that the Holy Spirit should inspire the writer to put this verse in between two passages about His glory.

"The glory of the latter house *[the church]* shall be greater than the former *[Israel]* says the Lord of hosts; and in this place *[the place where His glory is]* will I give peace *[shalom — total well-being]*, says the Lord of Hosts."

The latter house is the church, you and me who are believers in Christ. The former house is Israel or a reference to God's glory formerly being in Solomon's temple. It seems quite clear to me that if the Holy Spirit who inspired the writers of the Bible saw fit to sandwich a verse about wealth and riches in between two verses about the most holy and spiritual thing we can think of, God's glory, then He did it for a reason! I believe He was wanting us to realize that when God's glory comes to your house (not the physical address you live at but inside of you, the temple of God's Spirit) along with it comes the potential for blessing financially and prosperity. Just as Jesus' presence always brought blessing when He was here on earth and when He was with His servants like Joseph who I mentioned earlier, it will bring blessing and abundance to your life as well, if you will believe for it and expect it.

I am not a wealthy man in terms of how the world considers wealth, but I must say that the Lord has blessed me far above what I could have imagined and situated me for favor in many ways. He has more than met our need financially and given "the power to get wealth" (Deut. 8:18) when it seemed there was no obvious source.

Lastly, the Word of God is clear about giving unto the Lord His portion and the blessings that come on our lives when we do. Malachi 3 is the portion of scripture which not only outlines for us tithing but also the many blessings that come in association with it. Malachi 3:10-12:

"'Bring all the tithes into the storehouse, that there may be food in My house, and try Me now in this,' Says the Lord of hosts, 'If I will not open for you the windows of heaven, And pour out for you such blessing that there will not be room enough to receive it. 11 And I will rebuke the devourer for your sakes, So that he will not destroy the fruit of your ground, Nor shall the vine fail to bear fruit for you in the field,' Says the Lord of hosts; 12 'And all nations will call you blessed, For you will be a delightful land,' Says the Lord of hosts."

This is a portion of scripture and an aspect of our lives that the Lord clearly challenges us to do as He says and outlines what the divine results will be if we do!

Here is what He says He will do for us if we will do our part and give tithes (10% of our income) and offerings (above our tithes):

1. Open the windows of heaven and pour you out a blessing. That's favor! That's revival spiritually and blessing in all dimensions of your life.

2. You and I will be blessed with more than we can even handle. (abundance)

3. He will rebuke the devourer (Satan) In other words, when the enemy tries to eat up your seed like the birds or seedeaters do, He will stop him, paralyze him, and protect your finances and your seed sown. There will be a return on your giving or your sowing into God's Kingdom!

4. The fruit of your ground (your business or livelihood) will not be destroyed or harmed.

5. Your vine (your children) will have no lack and will be protected.

6. Nations shall called you blessed (you will be a testimony of God's goodness, faithfulness and blessing).

7. You will be a delightsome land (in other words, people will want what you have and He will use you to testify of His greatness, goodness and blessing).

All of these blessings come when you honor the Lord with your tithe or first fruits. I have proven this in my life as a Christian for many years and also as a Minister of the Gospel.

I would be remise if I didn't point out that Father Abraham, who we have more than established was a very blessed man in every way, was the original tither in the Bible.

"For this Melchizedek, king of Salem, priest of the Most High God, who met Abraham returning from the slaughter of the kings and blessed him, 2 to whom also Abraham gave a tenth part of all, first being translated 'king of righteousness,' and then also king of Salem, meaning 'king of peace,' 3 without father, without mother, without genealogy, having neither beginning of days nor end of life, but made like the Son of God, remains a priest continually. 4 Now consider how great this man was, to whom even the patriarch Abraham gave a tenth of the spoils" (Heb. 7:1-4).

Melchizedek is a type of Christ in the Old Testament; the King of Salem which means "the King of Peace". When the King of Peace (Jesus) is present in your life and you bring Him the tithe as Abraham did many generations ago, you will be blessed like he was, and abundance and prosperity will be yours in every way.

CHAPTER TEN

The Blessing of Supernatural Intervention and the Miraculous

One of the direct benefits of inheriting the Blessing of Abraham is the supernatural power of God to intervene in the tough battles we come up against in the spirit realm as well in the natural realm. The Word makes it very clear in Ephesians 6:12 that "…we wrestle not against flesh and blood, but against principalities, against powers, against the rulers of darkness of this world, against spiritual wickedness in high places." This type of warfare cannot be waged in our strength alone. We must have the supernatural intervention of the Holy Spirit to stand against these forces of wickedness because we are no match for them without His power.

Thankfully, part of our inheritance as believers is the divine ability to partner with the Spirit of the Lord against such demonic strongholds and bring them down in the authority and power of His Name. I love what Romans 8:26 says: "Likewise the Spirit also helps in our weaknesses. For we do not know what we should pray for as we ought, but the Spirit Himself makes intercession for us with groanings which cannot be uttered." If you look up the word "helps" in the Greek, the original language of the New Testament, you will find that it is the Greek word *sunantilambonamia* which means "to take hold together against." You may not remember that long Greek word but don't forget what it means because once you grasp this, you will have learned a powerful key to overcoming power in your spiritual walk. The Apostle Paul is saying, "You in participation and partnership with the Holy Spirit are an unbeatable force." You and I have the power to "bring down" the assault that has come against us in the spirit realm and see them defeated! PTL! We need to learn how to cooperate with the Holy Spirit and when the need arises, "take hold together against" a stronghold that has come to keep us defeated, discouraged and prevent us from realizing our victory in Christ.

Armed and Ready For Battle

The Lord didn't leave us defenseless against an enemy that is clearly stronger than we are in our own human strength. He gave us the weapons of warfare found in Ephesians chapter 6 which "are mighty through God to the pulling down of strongholds" as 2 Corinthians 10:4 tells us. Perhaps you've been dealing with a situation that no matter how much you've prayed about it, fasted, and called on the Lord to heal or fix it, yet nothing seems to change it. Pray in the Spirit! Why? That's the blessing of Abraham …the promise of the Spirit (Gal.3:14). Praying in the Spirit activates your authority and summons the Holy Spirit's assistance against this seemingly immovable obstacle standing in the way of your victory!

Pray In The Spirit, Jim!

My sweet Mom, who was a mighty woman of faith, would always say, "Pray in the Spirit, Jim!" when I would call her and start to tell her about a problem I was dealing with. She wasn't being insensitive to my need; she loved her sons more than words could say. But Mom had long before discovered the key to victory that unlocks the mighty power of God and connects you to "the Helper" or "the Comforter" who, with your participation, will bring about a supernatural intervention and an answered prayer. Many times in my walk as a Christian I have heeded that sound advice of my Mom, and it has brought me through very trying situations that in the natural almost caused me to give up in despair. The Holy Spirit is just waiting for you to call on Him. He is ready and able to bring down the spiritual forces, principalities, spiritual wickedness and powers we wrestle against, which are listed in Ephesians 6:12.

Several years ago a dear uncle of mine, my Uncle Frank, suffered a stroke that left him very incapacitated and totally dependent on his family for care. Uncle Frank was a man of the Spirit and in fact, I recall hearing the story when I was a young boy of how he had received the Baptism of the Holy Spirit while praying for his baby daughter, my cousin Barbara, when she had been taken with a raging fever. I happened to be ministering at several churches in New England in the fall of 2011 so I decided to drive down to Nutley, New Jersey, my home town, and visit my Aunt Esther and Uncle Frank before driving down to Tom's River, New Jersey to have a brief visit with my Mom.

When I arrived at my aunt and uncle's house, my dear Aunt Esther greeted me with these words, "We have a problem, Jim." I asked, "What's wrong? How can I help?" My Aunt had been caring for my uncle in their home after he had been discharged from the hospital. Uncle Frank wasn't a small man and Aunt Esther is a petite little lady who obviously didn't have the strength physically to move my Uncle from the bed to the chair, the chair to the bathroom and back to bed, etc. My cousin, Peter, had come by earlier and helped my Uncle out the bed but now several hours had passed and he needed and wanted to get back in bed. Through his slurred speech he said to my Aunt prior to my arriving, "Jimmy (that's what all my family members and childhood friends called me) will help me."

When I walked in the room, I greeted Uncle Frank with a kiss and then I told him I would try to help him back into bed. I am not a weakling but I was seriously wondering if I could lift him. Somehow, I put my shoulder under his arm and was able to shift him from the chair to the bed. After he was settled back in bed, he was moaning and saying words that were unintelligible. Aunt Esther and I were sitting next to him and just sharing about the situation but also about how the Lord had helped her through what was a very trying time. At a certain point in the conversation, I said to Aunt Esther, "Let's pray in the Spirit." Aunt Esther, of course, was eager to do that as she is woman of the Spirit. I have wonderful memories of her praying in tongues at the altar of our church in Nutley at our weekly prayer meetings.

The Spirit Man's Awareness

All of a sudden as we began to pray, Uncle Frank who had been groaning and moaning just a moment before, began to pray in the Spirit with us! I was awed at how, although his body and mind were very much disabled, his spirit immediately recognized the presence of the Holy Spirit and engaged! It was a powerful lesson to me that the Holy Spirit's presence and power inside us transcends the state of our natural man and can help us at our weakest state! Both my Aunt and Uncle hadn't been sleeping well for weeks since the stroke had occurred and not getting enough sleep along with all the challenges of his condition was only adding to a very difficult situation.

The next day, as I was about to board my flight from Philadelphia back to California, I got a call from Aunt Esther. She was rejoicing and said, "I just had to let you know that both Uncle Frank and I slept soundly last night and we feel so much better." Uncle Frank did go home to be with the Lord several months later but that divine visitation from the Spirit of the Lord was such a blessing and help! I will never forget how immediately Uncle Frank's whole demeanor changed and how "the peace that passes all understanding" (Phil. 4:7) filled that room and ministered to both him and my dear aunt that day! This, my friend, is part of our heritage as believers and as the inheritors of the Blessing of Abraham.

To further drive home this powerful truth, let me call your attention to the verse I referenced a moment ago, 2 Corinthians 10:4. In fact, let's take a closer look at what I believe the Apostle Paul was saying to the Corinthians and to us today. Here's what it says: "For the weapons of our warfare are not carnal, but mighty through God to the pulling down of strongholds." Verse 5 goes on to say, "Casting down imaginations [arguments] and every high thing that exalts itself against the knowledge of God, and bringing into captivity every thought to the obedience of Christ."

Partnership With The Holy Spirit

One day while meditating on this verse, the Holy Spirit opened up to me what I believe is an awesome revelation of this truth. I always believed that when Paul said the word "our" warfare, he was meaning us as the body of Christ. While I still agree with that, I believe there's a deeper meaning here when you look at the context of the verse. When he says "our" warfare, he does not only mean our in the collective sense of those of us who are part of the body of Christ; the "our" he's talking about is … us and the Holy Spirit! He's trying to make us aware of the tremendous power and authority we have when we use the weapons of "our" warfare together in cooperation with the Holy Spirit. This is how we truly can overcome against the powers of darkness and spiritual wickedness in high places. Together, when you activate the weapons of warfare by calling on the assistance of the Holy Spirit, He "causes us to triumph"

(2 Cor. 2:14). If we would only take advantage of what is at our disposal as spirit-filled believers, I believe we would see more demonstrations of the miraculous, intervening power of God!

A Visitation At The Midnight Hour

Sometimes your miracle, your breakthrough, your supernatural intervention may come at the midnight hour! We all would prefer instantaneous deliverance and answers to our prayers but often, as the saying goes, "God is never early, He's never late; He's always right on time!" If He has to, He'll send an angel your way to bring about your victory at the midnight hour! Take, for example, what happened when Paul and Silas prayed recorded for us in Acts 16:16-27.

There is an account in Scripture that takes place at the midnight hour. Let me set up the story for you. Paul and Silas were ministering and a young woman with a spirit of divination began following them day after day. Although she said good things about them such as, "These men are the servants of the most high God which show us the way of salvation," Paul recognized by the Spirit's discernment that she was not of God and cast the demon out of her and she was delivered immediately. However, her masters who realized that their hope of making a profit off of Paul's ministry were now gone (sadly this still happens in the ministry world today) brought them to the magistrates or rulers of the city and began spreading lies about them, saying they were causing trouble in the city.

Because of that, Paul and Silas were beaten with many stripes and were cast into prison. However, an amazing and miraculous thing happened when they began to praise and worship the Lord at the midnight hour! Verse 26 tells us that God heard their worship and brought about their deliverance "suddenly!"

Acts. 16:25-26 states, "And at midnight Paul and Silas prayed, and sang praises unto God; and the prisoners heard them. And suddenly there was a great earthquake, so that the foundations of the prison were shaken; and immediately all the doors were opened, and every one's bands were loosed."

A Lesson In Supernatural Intervention

Let me point out for you several amazing truths that we can gain from this incredible story. First of all, the Holy Spirit saw fit to include this testimony in the Holy Word of God! That tells me He wanted us to believe God for supernatural intervention!

Second, the Holy Spirit that was in the apostles gave them discernment to not be deceived by the seemingly praise-worthy words of this woman. Not everyone who says positive things about us is motivated by the Spirit of the Lord and sometimes their words can bring a snare if we are not praying in the Spirit for discernment and wisdom from the Lord.

Thirdly, God turned what seemed to be an "end-of-the-road" experience, a hopeless situation around for the Apostle Paul and Silas … when they began to praise the Lord. Although I have already spoken about this earlier, it bares repeating that praising the Lord gets heaven's attention and can bring about your answer in a supernatural way!

One of the Hebrew words for praise in the Bible is the little word *yada*. As I said in chapter one, the letters of the Hebrew alphabet are words with a meaning in themselves. If you breakdown the three Hebrew letters that this word *yada* is made up of, you discover a powerful truth. Hebrew reads right to left as opposed to left to write as the English language does. From right to left the three words are 1. yud (means hand or hands extended) 2. dalet (door) and 3. hey (that same fifth letter of the the Hebrew alphabet that God inserted into Abram's name making him Abraham which we have now learned means the Spirit of Grace and the breath of God.) The dynamic truth in this one little word for praise is this; when I lift my hands in praise *(yud)* to the Lord, the Holy Spirit *(hey)* opens the door *(dalet)* of blessing, grace and divine favor on my life resulting in supernatural intervention and assistance. I love that! God will meet us at the midnight hour like He met Paul and Silas and deliver us from our bondage, limits and dead-end experiences.

Fourthly, I love that the book of Acts uses the adverb "suddenly" and "immediately!" In fact, as you read the book of Acts, you see these words used often … suddenly this happened, immediately that happened and other synonyms like "straightway," which is old English for immediately. Somehow, in our day, we have been conditioned to believe that God's response to our prayer or our cry for help will take a long time. Perhaps it's because of what we've heard from our pulpits and various teachers of the Word; maybe it's because of tradition or church doctrine.

Take Off The Limits

I realize God is sovereign and His will for us is perfect but I must ask myself, "Why?" Perhaps you should as well. If God could and did supernaturally and suddenly intervene for the Apostles, why do we question His ability or willingness to do it for us today? Has God changed? Are our problems and difficulties too hard for God? Is anything too hard for God? Does He not love us as much as He loved them? The answer is an emphatic, "No!" His power is still the same and His Word is true and unchanging!

Expect God To Answer

I have said it often and I will say it again! It's time for the "suddenlies" (not a word I realize but you get the point) and the "immediatelies" (also not a word) to return to the body of Christ! It's time that we realize that as part of the blessing of Abraham, we can believe God and see miraculous answers to prayer. It doesn't have to take days, weeks, months or even years; it can happen suddenly! Amen! Perhaps that's why many have fallen away and left the church because they don't see the power that we speak of so often? Jesus often performed miracles before He taught His followers. Why? Because the miracles substantiated His authority and were a testament that He was who He said He was!

Our expectation has a lot to do with what we receive from the Lord! Sometimes we don't see answers because we are not expecting it to happen or have no faith that the answer will happen soon when we pray. Let's shake off that mindset and start expecting the supernatural intervention of God. When we do, I believe that we will start seeing more answers to prayer … suddenly!

A New Season of Blessing

Throughout the Old Testament and the New Testament, the Holy Spirit is likened unto breath and wind. In the Old Testament language of Hebrew it is the word ruach. In the New Testament language of Greek it is pneuma. In the first chapter of this book, I described for you one of the most powerful examples of what happens when God's Spirit breathes in a person's life and the transformation that happens following that encounter: The Blessing of Abraham (Gen.17:5).

HE is also represented by wind on many occasions throughout the Word of God. The most salient example of the New Testament would be Acts 2:2, which says, "And suddenly there came a sound from heaven as of a rushing mighty wind, and it filled the house where they were sitting." This is "the promise of the Spirit through faith" found in the latter part of Galatians 3:14 which describes what the Blessing of Abraham is.

I love what Isaiah 35 says about what happens when God's Spirit blows in our direction! One of my favorite Old Testament examples of the Holy Spirit being represented by wind is found in this passage. Keep in mind while reading this passage that there is a double prophetic application to it. The prophet Isaiah's ministry and prophecies reached all the way through time to the days of the Messiah (chapter 53) and down to our present time as we will soon discover. Before I read it, though, I'd like to share something from my growing up years in the state of New Jersey that reminds me of this passage and will help give a closer-to-home demonstration of this powerful prophesy.

Fragrance In The Air

After World War II, the Japanese government gave the United States a gift of the cherry blossom trees that now bloom in many of our US east coast cities as a reconciliatory gift. If you visit our nation's capitol in the springtime, you will see these glorious and colorful trees in full bloom gracing the parks of Washington, DC with not only their beauty but also their magnificent fragrance. Our towns in the area of northern New Jersey where I grew up, were fortunate enough to be blessed with many of these trees also. I can remember vividly that when we saw the cherry blossom trees begin to bud, then blossom, and release their lovely fragrance in the parks near my childhood home, it was a sign that a new season was beginning and the old, harsh winter season was ending. If it was a particularly windy day and the wind conditions were just right, you could smell that fragrance of the cherry blossom trees all over the town like a heavenly perfume. In a way, it brought hope ... hope that the long, hard, cold, miserable winter season was over and new life was springing up ... in a sense, like a healing was taking place and everything was coming back to life after a time of death, barrenness, and darkness.

Many years later, when I traveled to the land of Israel, I witnessed a similar occurrence that takes place every year in the Holy Land and is in particular what the prophet Isaiah is speaking of in chapter 35 of the book that bares his name.

Let me remind you of some geographical information that will help give context to the passage we are about to read. If you look at a map of the middle east, you will notice that Israel is situated directly south of the country of Lebanon, it's northern neighbor. In the springtime, just like as in the case of the cherry blossoms trees, the tall and mighty cedar trees which are abundant in the country of Lebanon begin to blossom and in like manner, give off a glorious, beautiful aroma and fragrance that fills the air. When the wind conditions are just right, the north winds blow south into the country of Israel and you can smell this wonderful scent throughout the Holy Land. With this in mind, let's read what the prophet wrote in Isaiah 35:1-2:

"The wilderness and the solitary place shall be glad for them; and the desert shall rejoice, and blossom as the rose. 2 It shall blossom abundantly, and rejoice even with joy and singing; the glory of Lebanon shall be given unto it, the excellency of Carmel and Sharon, they shall see the glory of the Lord, and the excellency of our God."

Prophecy Fulfilled

In the natural realm, the wilderness that Isaiah is referring to is the country of Israel, which is basically a desert where nothing can grow. Apart from their amazing ingenuity in developing a drip system of irrigation, it would still be barren and desolate today. Even today, as you drive down out of Jerusalem, which in every way is a modern-day city, within a very short distance you are in the desert, complete with nomads who live a very primitive existence just like they lived in Isaiah's time. The prophet is seeing generations before it happened, modern-day Israel which if you've been there you can testify to, has become an agricultural wonder. The desert is blossoming as the rose just as Isaiah prophesied centuries ago, so much so, that now, the country of Israel has become one of the major exporters of produce, and the produce that comes from Israel is some of the most excellent in quality in the world.

I have travelled to Israel more than 20 times and I have seen with my own eyes the fulfillment of Isaiah's prophesy. When the prophet says in verse two "the glory of Lebanon shall be given unto it" he is talking about that glorious fragrance that the cedar trees give off in the springtime and that permeates the atmosphere all throughout the Holy Land in the springtime when the north winds blow south. Just like with the cherry trees in our Capitol, when that fragrance fills the air in the Holy Land, it blows out the pollution and bad atmosphere and replaces it with a fresh, new quality of air. When that happens, suddenly things that were dormant, stagnant, desolate, barren, dry and unproductive, start to bud, bloom and bare fruit again. With the new season comes new life, glory and vibrancy that just days before seemed gone forever.

Revived And Reborn

What the prophet Isaiah is saying to us is this: when you see this happening in the natural realm, as we are definitely seeing today, pay attention! It will also happen in the spiritual realm. When the glory of God, represented by the glory of Lebanon in Isaiah's prophesy, blows south into your desert spiritually, a reviving of your spirit takes place and along with it will come a rebirth of that which you thought was dead. Dreams, visions and godly passions that until now have gone unfulfilled, start to come true. Hope returns and brings expectation that your prayers will be answered. It brings new life in your spirit and as you inhale His glorious fragrance, you breathe health, quickening power, reviving your spirit by His Holy Spirit. Suddenly, all that was dead, dying, and barren begins to come back to life and your spirit-man is reborn.

Perhaps you've been experiencing a long, dry and desolate season in your life spiritually and you've almost given up feeling as though it's hopeless. The Word of the Lord spoken through the prophet Isaiah in Isaiah 54:1 is also referred to by the Apostle Paul in his letter to the Galatians, found in Galatians 4:27, which says: "Rejoice, O barren, you who do not bear! Break forth and shout, you who are not in labor! For the desolate has many more children than she who has a husband."

In a moment's time, the Spirit of the Lord can blow into your desert experience and breathe life, supernatural intervention, miraculous power into your heart and life and change your season by His glory and presence. If you read on further in Isaiah chapter 35 you discover the results of God's glory coming to both a nation and a life are healing, deliverance, peace, abundance, divine intervention and protection and more. Let me pray with you and agree for these to happen in your circumstances today:

Prayer:

"Father God, I recognize that some who are reading this book may be facing what seems to be an impossible situation and they are desperately in need of Your Supernatural Intervention. As You proved Yourself faithful to Paul and Silas at the midnight hour, breathe the breath of Your Holy Spirit, the blessing of Abraham, the glory of Lebanon into their hearts right now, I pray, and bring about a reviving of hope, peace, grace and faith to believe You will show up in Your power and might to deliver. Blow, breath of God, and change their dry and barren season with a new atmosphere of life, health, peace and abundance. Amen."

The Blessing of Restoration and Recovery

Have you ever had something stolen from you? It's a very violating experience and after you get over the shock of the loss, anger can set in for the one who perpetrated the act!

I remember when I was a young boy growing up in New Jersey. We had a family get-together at our house which was on one end of our charming town of Nutley, across town from where many of my Mom's family lived and were my Mom had grown up. The city of Nutley is a lovely town, located about 30 minutes outside of New York City. In fact, when I was growing up I could see the New York skyline from my bedroom window. As the party was wrapping up and some of the family members had left, we were cleaning up the kitchen (there's always food involved in an Italian family gathering) and the phone rang. I happened to be the one who answered the phone which was hanging on the wall in our kitchen and heard my Aunt Esther, who had just gotten home from the party. From the tone in her voice, I could tell she was quite shaken up. "We've been robbed!" she said. I remember the feeling that went through me hearing those words, partly because of the fact that as a child, things make a big impact on you and partly because of my concern for my dear Aunt and Uncle and their family. I can still remember the anxiety in her voice to this day. Thankfully, despite the fact that the thieves took a few valuables, none of the family was home at the time and no one was harmed, other than being emotionally shaken up.

The Psalmist David, who became King of Israel went through a terrifying experience of loss and to make matters worse, not only David but all of his soldiers who had been away with him doing battle also lost their wives, children and all of their belongings when the Amalekites invaded their city, plundered it, and burned it to the ground. The chilling story is described in 1 Samuel 30. Thankfully, this story has a happy ending!

1 Samuel 30:1-6 describes the account. "Now it happened, when David and his men came to Ziklag, on the third day, that the Amalekites had invaded the South and Ziklag, attacked Ziklag and burned it with fire, and had taken captive the women and those who were there, from small to great; they did not kill anyone, but carried them away and went their way. So David and his men came to the city, and there it was, burned with fire; and their wives, their sons, and their daughters had been

taken captive. Then David and the people who were with him lifted up their voices and wept, until they had no more power to weep. And David's two wives, Ahinoam the Jezreelitess, and Abigail the widow of Nabal the Carmelite, had been taken captive. Now David was greatly distressed, for the people spoke of stoning him, because the soul of all the people was grieved, every man for his sons and his daughters" (NKJV).

The loss was so great, as it would be for anyone faced with such a devastating experience, that although David and the soldiers had been mighty and strong in battle, these grown men cried until they had no tears left to cry! Have you ever been there? I have and it's not pleasant! Imagine, he was not only grieving over his own personal loss of his wives, but on top of this, his men have turned on him and were so angry that they were talking about killing him!

Two Options

After you get over the emotional impact and shock of going through such an immeasurable loss, you have only two options: stay stuck in the shock stage, which leads to a deeper state of depression or get angry with the enemy that has inflicted the loss, pick yourself up, regroup, and go after what has been stolen, taking back what is rightfully yours! This is exactly what God told David to do!

I'm not advocating that anyone go after the "people" who have wronged you, but rather get angry at the source, the wicked one, who according to the Word in John 10:10 has come "to steal, and to kill, and to de-

204 • The Blessing: This is Your Time!

stroy!" Sometimes you just have to say to yourself, "Enough is enough; I'm taking back my stuff!" When the Spirit of the Lord comes on you, you rise in holy anger against the plots of the devil to destroy you, your family and begin to take back that which has been stolen. This, my friend is also part of the blessing on our lives as the children of Abraham; the Spirit's assistance in recovering that which has been lost or stolen from us.

David's Keys To Victory

"How do you do that," you ask? By doing what David did in the above mentioned story … that's how! "What did he do," you ask? The answer is found as you continue reading in 1 Samuel 30. "But David strengthened himself in the Lord his God" (1 Sam. 30:6).

Key 1: Strengthen Yourself In The Lord

In times of loss, the first thing to do is to strengthen yourself in the Lord as David did. We do that in several ways. Notice is says David "strengthened himself." When we experience heartache, loss and hardship, our first reaction is often to run to others for comfort, consolation and encouragement, which is good to a certain extent. Thank God for caring people who are there for us in our hour of need. However, nothing can take the place of knowing how to "come boldly to the throne of grace, that we may obtain mercy and find grace to help in time of need" (Heb. 4:16).

Take Refuge

Learn how to get into God's presence. Allow His Spirit to breathe recovery into your spirit, which will give you a renewing in your body, mind, and spirit, enabling you to pick yourself up along with all the shattered pieces of your life and go after that which has been stolen. In His presence, He will reveal His plan for the future and His promises about your future. "For I know the plans I have for you," declares the Lord, "plans to prosper you and not to harm you, plans to give you hope and a future" (Jer. 29:11, NIV).

The Path To My New Season

After I was launched into my new season of ministry in 2010, although I knew the Lord was in it and was definitely fulfilling what He had spoken to me about several years earlier in 2003, bringing me into a new season of ministry, I went through a very tough time emotionally because of the loss of something that I had cherished for over 22 years of my life. It was painful to have taken away from me, quite suddenly, my position, my work associates who were more like a second family, and my livelihood and source of income in a matter of days. I felt as though I was experiencing a death so to speak and was grieving just as one does when they lose a loved one. Yes, I will admit it! I cried and wept over the loss. But, thankfully, I have learned over the years how to strengthen myself as David, and the first place I ran to was the presence of the Lord.

For about the first three months of 2010 I experienced the comfort and fellowship of the Spirit in a glorious way each day as I would spend hours in prayer and reading the Word of God. Out of that painful time came glorious revelations of the Word such as the basic truth of this book, The Blessing, and I wouldn't trade it for anything. Not only that, but He breathed faith back into my spirit to believe that as painful as it was to let go of what had been dear to me, that if I trusted Him and stepped out in faith, He would "restore the years that the locust had eaten" as Joel 2:25 says and give me a future that was even more blessed and fulfilling than the season that had just ended. I often write in my journals and during that time, I filled several journals with not only my thoughts and heart's cry but also the revelations from God's Word that He gave me daily while in His presence. He literally breathed new purpose, new strategy for implementing my new season and new courage to believe God that my latter would be greater than the rest.

Now, looking back on that experience, as much as I loved that season of my life, there's no way that I would trade what I have experienced in the last five plus years and honestly wouldn't want to go back if that were somehow possible. Now when I stand to minister in my own services, the anointing that I experience as I preach the Word of God and as I minister in the gifts of the Spirit is powerful and awesome. I literally can sense Him ministering through me, and I know that it would not have happened unless I had let Him turn my loss into a glorious recovery.

I had to let go of the past, as glorious and wonderful as it had been, and trust that what was coming would be even greater. I remember I had the song "Moving Forward" written by Israel Houghton and sung by Ricardo Sanchez in my car CD player and in my cell phone, and I played it over and over to get its message deep into my spirit. Here are the lyrics:

*"I'm not going back, I'm moving ahead
Here to declare to You my past is over in You
All things are made new, surrendered my life to Christ
I'm moving, moving forward."*
— **words and music by Israel Houghton**

I wrote a note to Ricardo and thanked him for recording this song because the Holy Spirit literally breathed that message into my spirit and helped me to believe God for my future. That brings me to the second thing David did to bring about a recovery. When you find the secret place of the Most High, true worship begins to erupt from your spirit, releasing the peace of God and His abundance on your life.

Key 2: Encourage Yourself In the Lord

David praised and worshiped the Lord! As I have stated earlier, David was a worshipper of the Most High God and had a long history of praising God which is clearly expressed by the many Psalms that were written by him. David knew that one of the most certain ways to recovery and restoration was to magnify God, despite the circumstance. We see this in his conquest of the Philistine giant, Goliath recorded in 1 Samuel 17. David's response to the taunting and threats of this foul-mouthed, belligerent bully is "classic David" when he said in 1 Samuel 17:45: "You come against me with sword and spear and javelin, but I come against you in the name of the Lord Almighty, the God of the armies of Israel, whom you have defied." (NIV) David had learned that it's sometimes not enough to speak to God about your problem (in this case the giant Goliath who was threatening his and the entire nation of Israel's very existence) but you have to speak to the problem (the giant) about your God! What was David doing here? He was magnifying or praising the Lord rather than the problem or giant that was standing in his way and threatening his very survival.

Praise Puts Things Back Into Proper Perspective!

David's focus was not on the problem, aka Goliath; his focus was on the Lord Almighty evidenced by the last part of this verse. David had learned not to magnify the problem but rather to magnify the Lord. In so doing, the Lord gave him a divine strategy for defeating the enemy and for bringing about a victory. That's what praise will do! It becomes a mighty weapon in our hand as Psalm 149:6 says and paralyzes the giant or thing that threatens to destroy us, bringing it down.

Psalm 149:6 proclaims, "Let the high praises of God be in their mouth, and a two edged sword in their hand."

The above verse tells us two specific things that praise does. 1. It strengthens our hand (the word of God becomes a mighty weapon of warfare in our hands); 2. It paralyzes the enemy and stops him in his tracks!

When we praise the Lord, the Spirit of the Lord breathes hope and strength into us and makes the Word of God real and powerful in our hands. Then, in the power of the Spirit, we become able to use the Word, which is the sword of the Spirit, against the enemy to stop his attempts and bring restoration from the ashes of our lives.

The Path To Recovery

I asked you earlier if you have experienced loss in the past? Another great story of how praise brought about recovery and restoration is found in the book of Ruth. Naomi, Ruth's mother-in-law, understood something of what you may have gone through. Not only did she and her husband Elimelech have to move to Moab because of famine (lack, shortage, loss) but then soon after, her husband dies. Ten years later, her two sons die. Now that's loss! But Ruth 1:7 gives us insight into what was the beginning of her recovery. Scripture says they returned to Judah. Judah means praise also. The path to recovery is praise. The beginning of our restoration is praise. Praise sets in motion heavenly intervention. Praise prepares the heart to receive. Praise softens one's spirit to become receptive and submissive to the word and will of the Lord, thereby setting us up for favor.

Key 3: Look For a Word from the Lord and Agree with the Word of God

The third thing David was this: he looked for a Word from the Lord and agreed with the Word of God! "And David said to Abiathar the priest, Ahimelech's son, 'Please bring the ephod here to me.' And Abiathar brought the ephod to David" (1 Sam. 30:7).

Abiathar was the priest, a man of God and a man of the Word. David asks him to bring the ephod, which was an apron-like garment that priests wore over their garment. From its earliest forms and uses, it appears that the ephod was associated with the presence of God or those who had a special relationship with God. It is portrayed as a source of divine guidance, as in this instance when David wanted to know if he should pursue the Amalekites (1 Samuel 30:7-8). David found the guidance he was looking for and decided to pursue or go after those who had caused him and his men such a tremendous loss.

When you are seeking to bring about recovery from a loss, it is vital to go to the Word of God and in His divine presence, let the Lord breathe hope, encouragement, wisdom guidance and divine strategy into your spirit. However, it's not enough to just consult the Word; we must come into agreement with the Word in order for it to become a sword or weapon in our hands to take back what has been stolen and what is rightfully ours! This is why we must also surround ourselves with people who know the Word of God and will come into agreement in prayer with you to bring about your victory. Sometimes our friends and even family members, as well-meaning as they may be, can hinder our faith if they are not in agreement with the Word of God. Jesus had to dismiss the mourners out of the room when he prayed for Lazarus to be resurrected from the dead because He knew their faith level was not where His was. Make sure that those you confide in are people of faith and people that will agree with you rather than bring you down or discourage your faith for recovery and restoration!

Key 4: Pursue or Go After What Belongs to You!

If you read the story in 1 Samuel 30, you will see that in addition to the first three keys I have already given you, God gave him instruction to pursue the enemy (1 Sam. 30:9-10). What does that mean to us in our day? I believe it means go after the thing lost, whether it be a financial loss or a relationship loss or a spiritual loss in the Spirit, utilizing the power that has been given us in His Name, by His Word, through the weapons of warfare which are activated by the Holy Spirit.

Let me share another situation in my life where we experienced a loss but God miraculously brought about a recovery for my wife and me. You may recall, the years from 2000 to about 2008 were years of economic growth and many were "flipping" houses and making a substantial profit in doing so. We bought a rental property in a thriving area of California about an hour and 15 minutes from where we lived in Mission Viejo, California at the time. We were advised that it could be quite profitable and seemed like a good investment.

For a while, all was going along well until our tenant decided not to pay the rent. After having promised month after month that he would pay, he eventually skipped town without paying what he owed us. To make matters worse, they left what was a charming brand new house in horrible disrepair. Not only did we lose the rent money for six months but on top of that, we had to pay to remove the belongings they left behind, repair huge holes in the walls, paint the house and more. I have to be honest, I was mad! I wasn't mad at the Lord, and not so much mad even at these tenants who had taken advantage of us, but mad at the devil for robbing us. We amassed a debt of $10,000 in that six-month span related to the rental property, and I was not happy about it, to say the least!

Enough Is Enough!

You see, I have always been a person who tithes and not only given the ten percent of my income (and then our income after we married) but in addition, we have given offerings above and beyond our tithes. I believe what the Word says about tithing! Our finances have always been blessed and although we weren't rich, the Lord had always blessed us with lovely houses, nice cars and financial security for my family and me. Now, all of a sudden, wham! We got hit with the tsunami of financial pressure because of this $10,000 unexpected debt! What did we do? We went to the Lord about it, just like David did in 1 Samuel and started to believe God that we, like David, would "recover all!" Sometimes we Christians are too passive about what happens to us and the Lord is wanting us to do as David did … ask Him how to go after what is rightfully ours and take back what belongs to us. This is exactly what I determined to do because I was angry that the devil had stolen from me and in my spirit I said, "Enough is enough!"

Shortly after that, I was in a miracle crusade with Pastor Benny in Worcester, Massachusetts. In the morning service, Pastor Benny asked a preacher whom God has used to bring Christians into financial liberty and abundance to speak for about a half an hour. Now, I want to insert here, I have heard my share of preachers frankly manipulate people into giving a certain amount and make promises that in a week's time, they would receive a harvest, etc., and had been turned off by that as many of you reading this book have also probably been. I don't believe that gimmicks are ever appropriate when taking up an offering and quite frankly, I have seen enough that have sickened me and turned me off big time! That being said, I also realize that there is a divine principle involved in sowing seed into good ground and a blessing that can come to your life when you are obedient to the voice of the Lord when He lays it on you heart to give! So, I don't "throw out the baby with the bath water" as the expression goes!

This particular morning, I listened with an open spirit and mind to the preacher and the Holy Spirit spoke to my heart to give an offering of $1,000. Now, $1,000 to me at the time was like $10,000 or more to me and I honestly didn't even know how we would make it through the month financially because of an already strained budget. I remember going forward wondering, "Are you out of your mind, Jim?" But I knew that I had heard the Holy Spirit's voice so I obeyed.

God is my witness, just one week later I received a call from an associate to a pastor in Singapore, asking me to come and lead worship for a conference that they were holding at their church. Pastor Benny was one of the guest speakers, but he had decided because of the high cost involved in travel, etc., that he was not going to bring any of the usual staff which normally accompanied him on trips like this. But now, here I'm being asked to go … not at Pastor Benny's ministry expense, but at the expense of the host pastor.

God's Favor Demonstrated

I made the long trip to Singapore and wouldn't you know, my luggage did not arrive with me when I landed in Singapore. It was only a few hours until the first service began and I had no clothes to wear for the service except the ones on my back … certainly not appropriate for ministry. The staff of the host pastor were most gracious and quickly brought me to a shopping mall to buy a suit, shirt, shoes, etc., to wear that evening and would not let me pay for it either! Favor!

The conference was great and after the last service, I headed to the airport to catch a red-eye flight back to California where we were living then. On my way out of the church, the Associate Pastor, who had initially contacted me about coming, handed me a thick white envelope and said, "My Pastor wants you to have this." I was sort of surprised by it but since I was in a hurry to get to the airport, I said, "Thank you very much," proceeded to put it in my brief case, and left for the airport.

Restoration and Recovery

Several hours later, somewhere over the Pacific ocean, I woke up from sleeping for a few hours and I heard the Spirit of the Lord say to me, "Look inside the envelope." So, I pulled out my briefcase as quietly as possible, trying not to disturb the passengers around me. Then I turned on my light above my seat and opened the envelope. To my shock and amazement, I discovered the envelope contained $10,000 USD in crisp new hundred dollar bills! My heart was overjoyed when I realized that the Lord had not forgotten about our loss and had blessed my/our obedience in giving the $1,000, which I believe began a means of recovery for my wife and me after that tenant had left town without paying the rent they owed and left our house in shambles.

In the case of David and his men going after the Amalekites who had robbed them, once God told him to pursue, God brought him a bridge or a divine connection which helped him locate the enemy. The man happened to be an Egyptian slave of the Amalekites who had been left by his master because he was weak and sickly and in exchange for being an informant of where their mutual enemy was, David spares his life (1 Sam. 30:13-15). As the story goes, because of this "divine intelligence," David and his men were led to the exact location of where the enemy was and found them celebrating by eating and drinking with their defenses down. That night they overtook them and only 400 out of the thousands of Amalekite soldiers escaped and the rest were slain. Not only that, David and his men rescued their loved ones and took back ALL that had been stolen from them!

I believe that once we pray in the Spirit and allow the blessing of Abraham to breathe hope, divine strategy and faith into our hearts for recovery by the Word of God, He will bring us divine connections and divine favor that will help us regain that which we have lost just like in my case after having been robbed by the enemy when my tenant failed to pay rent for months and destroyed our rental property.

Joel 2:23 makes an amazing promise to anyone who has suffered loss and is needing restoration: "And I will restore to you the years that the locust hath eaten, the cankerworm, and the caterpillar and the palmerworm, my great army which I sent among you."

If you've read the book of Joel in the Bible and studied it like I have, you have discovered that one of the main themes of the book is restoration. In fact, here are the seven basic headlines of the book that demonstrate God's desire to bring recovery and restoration, even when some of the loss is the result of our own rebellion and disobedience!

Judgment / Call to prayer and fasting / Repentance (or turning around) / Supernatural Intervention / Restoration / Prosperity / Salvation and Deliverance.

God is in the business of recovery and restoration! Some paint Him to be a God full of wrath just waiting to pounce on us if we mess up in the slightest but even here in the Old Testament, prior to the age of grace that we now are living in, He showed Himself to be more than willing to forgive, to allow judgment to be averted and to provide a path to restoration and abundance.

It is also interesting to note that one of the most prophetic passages of scripture is found in Joel 2:28. It is a reference to the blessing of Abraham…the promise of the Spirit (Gal.3:14).

Joel 2:28 says, "And it shall come to pass afterward [after the Holy Spirit of Grace or the Blessing of Abraham] that I will pour out my Spirit upon all flesh; your sons and your daughters shall prophesy, your old men shall dream dreams, your young men shall see visions."

God wants to pour out His Spirit and replace our devastation, our loss and destruction with His abundant grace and favor! This promise is not just for the church in general but I believe it is a promise to each of us individually.

I don't know what loss you've experienced, my friend, or how it may have caused you tremendous emotional pain and despair. However, I do know this: God wants to give you the testimony of David! He wants to bring beauty out of the ashes of your life, give you the oil of joy for mourning and the garment of praise for the spirit of heaviness (Isaiah 61:1-3). I refer to this passage as "God's Divine Exchange Plan." Not a bad deal, aye?

While the Bible doesn't promise that all will be a bed of roses and that we as Christians will never experience hardship, trials, or tests of our faith, a recurring theme in both the Old and the New Testament is that our God is a God of restoration and recovery.

When the Spirit of the Lord, the Blessing of Abraham is on your life, I truly believe He will situate us for favor and for recovery from our losses if we will do as David did in 1 Samuel 30:19. Our testimony can be "_____(insert your name here) recovered all!"

CHAPTER TWELVE

The Blessing of Divine Protection

Have you ever been in a situation where you suddenly became aware of God's divine protection on your life? Was there a time when you knew beyond a shadow of doubt that God had supernaturally stepped in and protected you in a very dangerous and harmful situation, preventing tragedy and devastation? But how many times are we not aware of His watching over us, and yet He still shielded us from a tragic outcome? Sadly, when everything is going great, all too often one can become complacent and forget to give thanks for the blessing of God's divine protection that we some times take for granted. God has always protected His children, that is clearly demonstrated in both the Old and the New Testaments. We should remember to give thanks to Him for the blessing of divine protection is promised to us and to our loved ones.

There have been many times in my life that without a doubt, I have witnessed the supernatural intervention of God in protecting me, my family members, or my co-workers. I believe that this is part of the blessing that is ours in Christ Jesus as children of Abraham.

There are many passages in both the Old and New Testaments that declare to us as believers that as His children and subsequently, those of faith who are "blessed with faithful Abraham" (Gal. 3:9) we have the promise that in times of danger we will be shielded and divinely protected by the hand of God. Let me give you a few examples.

Exodus 12 gives us a description of the instructions God gave Moses so that they would be protected from the tenth and final plague He would send upon the Egyptians, who held the Israelites as captives and slaves. This was the most harsh plague of all in that the firstborn of every Egyptian household would be killed when the death angel passed by their house. In order to be protected while still living in Egypt (a type of the sin and the world) they were to kill a lamb on the tenth day of that month and apply the blood to the two side posts and the upper door post of their houses (a foreshadowing of cross of Jesus). When the death angel passed by, if the blood was applied to that house, they were divinely protected from harm and the firstborn lived. "And the blood shall be to you for a token upon the houses where you are: and when I see the blood, I will pass over you, and the plague shall not be upon you to destroy you, when I smite the land of Egypt" (Ex. 12:13 KJV). The Jewish people have celebrated this event called The Passover ever year since then. The blood of Jesus, applied to the door of our hearts, our households, our families, businesses, finances and every aspect of our lives, provides protection from all harm sent by the devil. Many of us have home and auto insurance, health insurance and so forth so that we will be protected in case of an accident, major disaster or health event. The best insurance however, is the blessed assurance of knowing you are "covered" by the blood of Jesus; it's comprehensive and there is no term limit!

Exodus 13:21 says, "And the Lord went before them by day in a pillar of a cloud, to lead them the way; and by night in a pillar of fire to give them light; to go by day and night." If you know anything about that part of the world which is mainly desert, during the day, the sun can be scorching and unbearable. The cloud not only was for their guidance but also provided a layer of protection from the harsh rays of the sun as they journeyed the long hours through the wilderness. The opposite extreme is also true in the dessert; at night, the temperatures drop to almost freezing and so the pillar of fire provided warmth during the long cold nights.

Exodus 14 describes the account of when the Egyptian army was pursuing the children of Israel. God instructs Moses to stretch out his hand with the rod in it and the Red Sea divided so they could pass through unharmed and escape the enemy. Once they were safely on the other side, God instructed him once again to stretch out his arm with the rod in it and the waters closed back in on the Egyptians and they were all drowned. At their darkest hour with no where to turn,

God gave them a miracle of divine protection and came through for them. Here's an interesting footnote to this Biblical story: archaeologists have recently discovered the remains of the Egyptian army in the exact location of the sea where this mighty deliverance took place!

2 Chronicles 20 gives us the account of when the Moabites and the Ammonites came against Jehoshaphat, King of Judah (when the Israelites were divided into two factions). At first, like is often our reaction, Jehoshaphat fears but after he receives the word of the Lord (the Word always brings courage and dispels fear) he rises up in the strength of the Lord and God miraculously gives him a tremendous victory. "Be not dismayed by reason of this great multitude; for the battle is not yours, but God's" (2 Chron. 20:15) He instructs the singers to praise (praise will always bring about your victory) and God does something amazing as a result of their praise. The Lord sends ambushments against the enemy and in their confusion, the armies kill one another, and God's people are divinely protected. I will share more about this in the next chapter.

A Shield of Protection

The Psalms are a tremendous reinforcement to this truth that God protects His own.

Throughout my life and especially over the past 40 years of ministry as I have traveled almost 4 million miles by air alone, in some very dangerous places on the earth, I have relied on the promises in the Word of God like the ones I am about to give you, for protection for not only me, but my family while I was away from them.

He has blessed me with a shield of His protection, and I am grateful to Him for it.

Psalm 3:3 says, "But You, Oh Lord are a shield for me; my glory and the lifter of my head." The presence of the Lord in our lives, or His glory, becomes a shield around us protecting us from danger and harm.

Psalm 23: 4-5 says, "Yea, though I walk through the valley of the shadow of death,

I will fear no evil; For You are with me; Your rod and Your staff, they comfort me. 5

You prepare a table before me in the presence of my enemies; You anoint my head with oil; My cup runs over."

Psalm 34:7 tells us, "The angel of the Lord encamps all around those who fear Him, And delivers them."

Psalm 42:1 says, "As the deer pants for the water brook, so my soul longs after Thee." There's a reason why the deer pants for and tries to get to the water. It's not just because it's thirsty either! The deer is panting because he is running frantically towards the water to escape its predator. Why? What's so special about the water? The deer knows instinctively that if he gets to the water, in the water, the predator will lose its scent and will no longer be able to track him. There, in the water, he will be protected and shielded from harm. The Psalmist was saying, this is just like what happens when we get into the presence of the Lord. There's a place of protection in God's presence, where like in the waters the deer is protected, we are divinely protected from the predator, Satan and shielded by God's glory. The Psalmist is encouraging us to do just as the deer does ... run to the water of His grace and glory and find protection.

Just like the deer can finally relax knowing it has escaped the predator's snare, so we find a rest in Him knowing we are protected in the secret place of the Most High as Psalm 91:1 states.

Psalm 91:1-10 says, "He that dwells in the secret place of the Most High shall abide under the shadow of the Almighty, ² I will say of the Lord, He is my refuge and my fortress; my God; in Him will I trust. ³ Surely He shall deliver me from the snare of the fowler [Satan] and from the noisome pestilence [like Ebola virus when I was recently in Western Africa and enterovirus that is presently here in the United States]. ⁴ He shall cover me with His feathers and under His wings you will trust; His truth will be your shield and buckler. ⁵ You shall not be afraid of the terror by night; nor for the arrow that flies by day. ⁶ Nor for the pestilence that walks in darkness, nor for the destruction that destroys at noon. ⁷ A thousand will fall at your side and ten thousand at your right hand but it will not come near you. ⁸ Only with your eye will you behold and see the reward of the wicked. ⁹ Because you have made the Lord, which is my refuge, even the most High your habitation. ¹⁰ There will no evil befall you; no plague will come near your house."

1 Peter 1:5, "Who are protected by the power of God through faith for a salvation ready to be revealed in the last time."

2 Thessalonians 3:3, "But the Lord is faithful, and He will strengthen and protect you from the evil one."

1 Corinthians 10:13 says, "No temptation has overtaken you but such as is common to man; and God is faithful, who will not allow you to be tempted beyond what you are able, but with the temptation will provide the way of escape also, so that you will be able to endure it."

These passages above are more than enough to convince me that as part of our inheritance as the children of Abraham, there is provided divine shielding and protection; we need to ask for it, expect it and believe for it. Let me give you a few examples of it in my personal life and as well in my professional ministry life.

One example occurred early on in ministry when I was a Music Minister at a church in Bangor, Maine. At the time I was single and away from my dear family in New Jersey. For holidays I would make the nine-hour trip down route 95 south from Bangor to be with my family, leaving after work. By the time I got on the road, it was already getting dark and the roads would typically be congested with everyone else was also heading out of town to be with their loved ones too.

After driving for several hours and struggling to stay awake, I dozed off. I don't know how long I was asleep … it may have been just moments … but when I awakened, I found myself heading down an exit ramp at nearly 60 miles per hour! Furthermore, I was heading straight for a car in front of me that was stopped at the bottom of the exit ramp. I slammed on my brakes and came to a sudden stop just inches from the car. As I took in everything that had just transpired, I knew without a shadow of a doubt that the Lord had protected me by His grace and spared me from an accident.

Up Close and Personal

It's one thing when you are the one who has been involved in accident or has been spared injury or death, but when it's your child, it's another matter altogether! I can say this from personal experience. When our precious son, Daniel, was just a small boy he attended the Christian Academy that was a part of the church where I was the Music Minister in Orlando, Florida. Several days a week after school the soccer team would practice in a field adjacent to the school property. At a set time, my wife, Mindy, would make her way to the school and wait in the line up of cars to pick up Daniel after practice was done.

One day as Mindy was waiting in her vehicle in the line up of cars, what she was about to witness is any mom or dad's worst nightmare! We had taught Daniel to always look both ways before crossing the street to be sure there was no oncoming car, and he was always careful to do just as we had instructed him to do. On the day in question he looked to the right and then to the left, but when he stepped out to move toward our car, all of a sudden a girl who was a new driver pulled out unexpectedly, and the next thing Mindy saw was the body of our precious son flying over the hood of the car and then sliding down off the hood to the ground. Imagine my wife's horror at that moment as she watched our precious son being catapulted through the air! Immediately, Mindy jumped out of the car and ran to Daniel's aid, not knowing what condition he was in at the moment. At the same time the school principle ran to my office, which was located in the adjacent building.

As the principle burst through the doorway of my office he said, "Everything is okay, Pastor Jim, but Daniel has been hit by a car."

I didn't wait for another word! The principle no sooner got the words out of his mouth and I ran like an olympian sprinter to the pick-up location, simultaneously praying in the Spirit and believing God for His supernatural protection and intervention on behalf of my son. I didn't know what to expect, but I knew that I could trust God in this instance just as I had trusted Him so many times before. Moments later I saw Mindy and Daniel, and to our amazement, Daniel was completely unharmed! Apart from being shaken up by the accident, there was no major injury to his body.

The paramedics were called as a precaution. When they arrived, they immobilized him just to be sure there were no internal injuries. From Mindy's eye-witness description of the accident, it was evident that Daniel had been divinely protected by the Lord, and his life was spared that day!

The scripture that I have held onto since I was a child and that I listed above, Psalm 34:7 that says, "The Angel of the Lord encamps around them that fear Him," became very real to us once again that day we knew with certainty that the Angel of the Lord had surely surrounded our son, Daniel! He is now 26 years of age, married, and a wonderful young man of whom Mindy and I are so proud.

This, my friend, is part of the blessing that belongs to you and me as believers. It is part of the blessing of Abraham that has been transferred to us as the children of Abraham and as joint heirs with Christ Jesus.

A Miracle In Venezuela

As I stated earlier, having been involved in an international traveling ministry for over 40 years, I can recall a number of situations where God's divine protection was visibly at work. One example that comes to mind took place in Venezuela in 2007. Our flight landed in Caracas well after darkness had fallen, and our flight arrangements made it impossible for our team to continue on by air to the city where we were scheduled to minister. Consequently, our host had organized two vehicles to pick us up and drive us the remaining three hours to Valencia where the event was to be held.

After we landed, we collected our bags and connected with the drivers who had come to pick us up. Three of us were traveling together so we were separated into two different vehicles. As we left the airport shortly after midnight, a misty rain began to fall. I was riding in the second vehicle. About an hour into the trip, we came to a winding stretch of highway that curved back and forth between various elevations of the terrain. We were traveling on a two-lane divided highway with a concrete wall separating us from oncoming traffic. The concrete retaining wall was average height, rising approximately to the base of the car windows. My friends, David and

Sheryl Palmquist, were in the first vehicle and I was riding in the second car. I was trying to make conversation with my driver, using my limited Spanish to converse.

As we were driving along in the darkness of night on the winding highway, an 18-wheel flatbed truck passed our vehicle and pulled up along side the compact car in which the Palmquists were riding. Suddenly and in mid-sentence of our conversation, I looked up to see the car carrying the Palmquists erratically swerving back and forth a few feet in front of us. I couldn't believe my eyes! Everything was happening so fast, and from my perspective, it looked like the car ahead of us was going to flip over because the highway had suddenly become slippery because of the mist. At almost the same moment, the road began to curve from left to right in an S-curve at that spot as well as sloping down hill as the highway continued to curve back and forth. As the driver tried to regain control of his swerving vehicle in the midst of these combined conditions, the right side of the car slid toward the flatbed 18-wheeler and slammed into the tires of the truck.

A Prayer of Desperation

I began praying and crying out the name of Jesus on behalf of my friends as I watched what was happening right in front of me in disbelief. The car slammed up against the truck and bounced off the huge truck tires. If the truck had been a few feet farther ahead, the car carrying the Palmquists would have been pulled under the truck. As the car bounded off the truck tires it careened to the other side of the roadway, slamming up against the cement divider and forcing the front and back tires on the left side of the car up onto the cement wall as the car was propelled forward. As soon as the driver was able to disengage the tires from the top of the cement wall, the car skidded off the cement wall and back across the lane toward the flatbed 18-wheeler again that was still traveling in the right lane. It was like watching an action movie unfold before me ... yet, it felt like it was happening in slow motion ... and I knew my friends and co-workers were in that vehicle!

When You Call, He Will Answer

I watched as I continued to call on Jesus for help ... perhaps much like the disciples did when they feared the waves would capsize their boat on the Sea of Galilee. I don't recall how many times the car bounced off the cement divider wall, but each time it did, there was a danger that it would be swept under the 18-wheeler in the next lane or flip and roll on the highway. After what seemed like several minutes, the driver was finally able to gain control of the car and bring it to a halt next to the cement divider. My driver pulled up behind the car and stopped the car. The vehicle was bent and the wheel well was caved in around the front tire, making it impossible to drive the vehicle.

By this time it was 1:00 a.m. or later, and we still had a distance to drive to reach our destination. The owner of the car quickly got out to set up some reflectors around the car to avoid being hit. Then he walked around the vehicle to check the damage. We were all speechless at what had just happened. In the moments before the car came to a halt, it was like everything was happening in a slow-motion ... and at the same time, everything was happening too fast to take everything in. All we could do was call upon the Lord for His divine protection and intervention in the situation. He guided the car safely to rest, even though it was too damaged to be driven. Everyone was shaken up but no one was injured. In that moment of need, God's divine protection delivered us from what could have been a very different outcome. We arrived in Valencia in the early morning hours ... our hearts filled to overflowing with gratitude for God's protection and knowing we had seen God's divine protection over our lives in action.

The Victory That Followed

The miracle didn't end with God's divine protection on that winding Venezuelan highway, which rescued my friends and co-workers from danger and injury. After a few hours rest, my co-workers and I were privileged to be part of an awesome outdoor miracle service, which was the reason we had all traveled to Venezuela. During that service it was as if God put His signature on the evening in a way that would always serve as a reminder to the Palmquists and me of His divine protection upon our lives. At one point in that service I saw one of the most amazing miracles that I have ever seen and it unfolded right before my eyes. I have seen many miracles during nearly three decades of ministry, but this was a miracle that I will never forget.

A young woman ... 23 years of age ... who had been paralyzed from the waist down three years earlier during childbirth, was miraculously healed. We learned that two of her friends had brought her to the service, trusting God to touch her. Because she was paralyzed from the waist down, she could not stand or walk, so she had arrived on a gurney or stretcher-like apparatus. At one point in the service, the anointing for miracles blew into that stadium like a fresh breeze. As she was lifted off the stretcher and assisted to stand, she slowly began to regain the feeling in her legs. As the feeling returned to her once-paralyzed legs and her legs became stronger, she was able to stand. In almost the same moment, she was so overcome with gratitude that she fell to her knees, lifted her hands and tears of joy flowed down her face as she praised God in Spanish. It was a beautiful sight that I will never forget!

Moments later with the help of the translator, she told the crowd that after she gave birth to her daughter, her husband left her because he couldn't deal with her paralysis. With no husband and unable to care for her child, she was forced to live with her family to help care for her and her child. In the three years since the birth of her daughter she said she had never carried her daughter.

A Visible Transformation

The next night she returned to the service to testify of God's healing power. When I first saw her, I didn't even recognize her because she didn't look like the same person. The first night she had been wearing a torn T-shirt, some sweat pants, and a pair of socks because someone brought her on a gurney because she couldn't walk or stand. However, the second evening her whole countenance was different. She was dressed in a beautiful red dress and wearing a new pair of metallic shoes. Her hair was clean with every hair in place. Her radiant smile beamed with joy as she carried her little girl in her arms and testified about what God had done in her body. She received a miracle that transformed her life and her daughter's life forever!

As a parent, my heart was so moved to see her joy as she held her daughter in her arms, hugging and kissing her. As a minister of the gospel, I was also moved, because standing before me was a tangible example of why we had come to Venezuela, enduring the long flights and traveling the final miles on a winding highway in the darkness that almost ended in an accident. I looked at the young woman and her daughter ... then shifted my gaze to David and Sheryl Palmquist who were also on the platform witnessing the miracle before us ... and we were all weeping tears of joy and gratitude at God's faithfulness. It was a moment that is forever etched on my memory.

Divine Protection To Do God's Work

Throughout the past almost 40 years that I travelled constantly around the globe to far away places like South Africa, West Africa, Australia, India, Russia, Europe, Malta, Israel and many more countries, God's faithfulness of divine protection has been very evident. As I'm writing this book, a number of world happenings like the Ebola virus outbreak in several West African countries has made international travel to places I've been before even more dangerous than ever.

In late 2014 I was scheduled to speak at a conference and several churches in Nigeria for five days. With the headlines and news agencies focused on the reports of the World Health Organization regarding the growing problem at the same time I was preparing to leave for Nigeria, I must admit, it did give me pause and I seriously contemplated rescheduling my ministry trip in light of the potential health risk for me and my family, not to mention all those with whom I come in contact with in the course of ministry. Watching news reports about this, plus the danger that ISIS and other terrorist organizations like Boko Haram pose in Africa and to those in the West with their stated goal of taking over America and attacking us on our home soil, can be very unsettling, to say the least. In fact, it could make one want to just bunker down and stay in your home with the doors sealed and locked!

I must admit, I went back and forth about my trip to Nigeria for several days ago. After much prayer and going to the Word, which is "a light unto my path" (Ps. 119:105), I decided that I must trust in the fact that the Lord, Who is omniscient (all-knowing) was aware that this would be occurring when I accepted the invitation and while not throwing caution to the wind as the saying goes, I had to go in faith believing Psalm 91:10 which promises, "No evil shall befall me; no plague [including Ebola or any other disease] shall come near my dwelling." I must stay ever conscious of the fact that as part of my inherited blessing from Father Abraham, I have received the Spirit of the Lord as a shield (Ps. 3:3) and I go about my daily routine and travel schedule in perfect peace, knowing that I am divinely protected.

God's Promise To Those Called By His Name

Make no mistake about it, the Bible is clear, "In the last days [and unless you've been living under a rock, there's no doubt we are in the last days before Christ returns] perilous times will come." However, the good news is that from even a cursory reading of the Old and New Testaments alike, one salient truth is the fact that throughout history: God has always protected His people

In Numbers 21:8 the Lord told Moses, "Make a snake and put it up on a pole; anyone who is bitten can look at it and live." Then God kept His promise for it says in verse 9 "When anyone was bitten by a snake and looked at the bronze snake, they lived." The snake or serpent was a divine foreshadowing of Jesus being lifted up on a Cross for you and me. Anyone who looks to the Cross will be saved … not just their souls, but their bodies, minds and total man. Don't fear Ebola or ISIS or any other deadly thing that may try to bite you or overtake you; look to the Cross and you will live!

Are You Covered?

We all have home and auto insurance so that we are "covered" and protected against loss in case of an accident or a catastrophic event. Regardless of how good the coverage is or how many pages are filled with the details of the protection provided by your insurance policy, it can't compare to the promise of the divine protection that belongs to the child of God. Exodus 12:13 says, "And the blood shall be to you for a token upon the houses where ye are: and when I see the blood, I will pass over you, and the plague shall not be upon you to destroy you, when I smite the land of Egypt." Cover your house, not just your physical dwelling place, or your car, but you, the temple of the Holy Spirit and your family members with the blood of Jesus, and every plague, including Ebola or any other deadly disease, will pass over you because "you're in good hands" when Jesus' blood covers you.

I read recently that scientists are now saying that the Ebola virus can be contracted from the tiniest drop of bodily fluid from an infected person. Dear reader, we have no cause to fear Ebola or any other deadly virus or disease because we are covered! What a wonderful assurance we have as God's children to know that just one drop of Jesus' precious blood is more powerful than any virus or disease of the body or cursed thing from the enemy.

Declare the verses listed in this chapter about divine protection over yourself, your family, your health, finances, your business, and every aspect of your life and believe that under the shadow of the cross of Jesus, you are continually protected from harm. Remember ... the cross transfers the blessing of Abraham on our lives, which includes divine protection.

The Blessing of "Another" or a Different Spirit

As I study the Bible, it becomes very evident that those who have had an encounter with the Spirit of the Lord like Abraham did were changed, and the transformation encounter made them different from that point on in their lives. Even in my own life, when I received the baptism of the Holy Spirit in 1968, I knew from that moment on that I would give my life in full time service to the Lord and was called to do His work. That experience made me somewhat different from my classmates and even as a teenager prior to entering Bible College, my heart was more about ministry, singing in churches all over our local area as well as becoming the president of our "C.A." youth group (Christ Ambassadors was the name of the Youth Departments in Assembly of God churches) than some of things that the average teenager is preoccupied with.

There's a powerful scripture in Numbers 14:24 which describes another less spoken of but none-the-less awesome man of God, Caleb. "But My servant Caleb, because he has a different spirit in him and has followed Me fully, I will bring him into the land where he went, and his descendants shall inherit it" (Num. 14:24 NKJV). The King James Version uses the word "another" in place of the word "different" but I believe different is a more accurate translation from the original text.

You will remember that Moses, the leader of the Children of Israel sent 12 men up into the Promised Land, or what was then called "Canaan," to spy on the enemies there and see whether or not they could conquer it and take possession of what God had promised them. Ten spies came back with a negative report; they only saw the obstacles, the giants and their perspective was totally different from the remaining two, Joshua and Caleb. These two men had a different spirit than the rest and were not deterred like the others; they possessed an over-comers mindset rather than a defeatist attitude like the others.

The word used here in Hebrew for another spirit is the very same word hey or hei, the fifth letter of the Hebrew alphabet that breathed into Abraham in Genesis 17:5. The same Blessing of Abraham had breathed into Caleb making him one of the two spies, along with Joshua who, upon returning from their espionage of the promised land, gave a positive report in contrast to the negative report that the other ten spies gave. The others saw giants and saw themselves as "grasshoppers" in comparison to the giants, but not Caleb and Joshua; they saw a land "flowing with milk and honey" and said to Moses and the others who were going on and on about not being able to conquer the land, "Let us go up at once and occupy it, for we are well able to overcome it." From that statement alone, we get a glimpse of just how different this man Caleb was from the rest. So the question arises, just how was he, and also those who likewise have the Spirit of the Lord or the blessing of Abraham in them, different?

Here are some amazing observations about people who have another Spirit or a different Spirit like Caleb had … people who know and have experienced The Blessing of Abraham.

Number 1. They See Things Differently!

When God's Spirit has breathed in you, you see things differently than the rest. You see yourself as a victor, not a victim. You look past the obstacles that stop everyone else and you push forward to receive all that has been promised to you by the Lord! You see setbacks as set ups for a comeback!

In the classic story of David and Goliath, David wasn't focused on Goliath, standing in front of him, spewing out his threats. No, he saw his God, bigger than this belligerent beast and David was confident that He would make him victorious in the end. The other soldiers cowered in fear at the sight of this Philistine; you can hardly blame them when you read this description of him in 1 Samuel 17:4-7: "And a champion went out from the camp of the Philistines, named Goliath, from Gath, whose height was six cubits and a span [over

9 feet tall]. 5 He had a bronze helmet on his head, and he was armed with a coat of mail, and the weight of the coat was five thousand shekels of bronze [about 125 pounds]. 6 And he had bronze armor on his legs and a bronze javelin between his shoulders. 7 Now the staff of his spear was like a weaver's beam, and his iron spearhead weighed six hundred shekels; [about 15 pounds] and a shield-bearer went before him." Whoa! Quite the imposing figure to say the least! David, however, saw things completely different from his fellow comrades.

David didn't see all that! He saw his God looming greater, mightier and larger than the beast named Goliath standing in front of him, arrayed in heavy armor that we just read about. Why? He had a different spirit! David had a relationship with the Lord and trust in Him that had been proven in the fields when he was growing up as a shepherd boy.   David didn't have the spirit of fear that others had and because of that he was able to kill a lion and a bear with his bare hands. He knew that if his God could give him the power to destroy these wild animals, this uncircumcised Philistine wouldn't be too hard for God!

Our problem often is that we have an incorrect perspective on the situation and because of that, we fail to receive the blessings that come from having a larger vision of the mighty God we serve.   How large is your vision of the Lord? Do you see Him greater than the problem or have you allowed the spirit of fear to magnify the problem so much that you feel dwarfed by it? Do you see Him as the One that is in you ... greater than the attack of the enemy that wants to destroy you? Do you see His ability to provide greater than your obvious lack? How you see Him and how you see yourself in Him matters! It makes all the difference in what you receive from Him.

When the Spirit of the Lord is present, you have supernatural vision to see beyond the problem, obstacle, giant or mountain to your God's almighty power.

The story of King Jehoshaphat in 2 Chronicles, chapter 20 further bares this truth out. Like King Jehoshaphat, you may not know what to do about the multitude of problems and the enemy that is battling against you. If you've read the account, you will recall that the Moabites and the Ammonites, two of Israel's enemies, came against Jehoshaphat in battle. When Jehoshaphat received word of the invasion, his first response was much like ours when an evil situation comes against us; he became fearful! Fear can be crippling and that is exactly what happened to him; he became paralyzed with fear and soon afterwards, despair set in.

If we are not careful, the enemy of our souls will magnify the problem so much in our minds that fear grips our hearts and soon we're paralyzed by it. The antidote for fear is faith! Faith in God is the only thing that will turn the situation around and cause you to triumph in the end. This is why it is so important that we are careful about what words we receive in our spirit because words can either bring life or death, liberty or bondage, victory or defeat.

Jehoshaphat calls on the Lord and calls for a fast in all Israel for divine intervention; it is from this moment that the situation begins to turn around. If you read the chapter, you will see that in verses 6 through 9 he begins to remind the Lord of their history with him, or in other words, their long heritage of faith and trust in God. In so doing, he is also building up his faith and reminding himself of the faithfulness of God in the past. In times of distress and battle, we should do the same.

Suddenly, the problem that seemed so insurmountable just moments before begins to become small in comparison to the greatness of your God. This is exactly what happened to Jehoshaphat.

The Spirit of the Lord comes on the prophet Jehaziel, and he begins to prophesy to Israel and specifically to their King Jehoshaphat saying, "Be not afraid nor dismayed by reason of this great multitude, for the battle is not yours but God's" (vs. 15). He goes on to prophesy in verse 17, "You shall not need to fight in this battle: set yourselves, stand still, and see the salvation of the Lord with you, O Judah and Jerusalem: fear not, nor be dismayed; tomorrow go out against them: for the Lord will be with you." When his eyes turn from the problem to the Lord, suddenly his whole attitude changes and he goes from FEAR to FAITH. His eyes are shifted off of the problem and onto the Lord for he says in verse 12, "For we have no power against this great multitude that is coming against us, nor do we know what to do, but our eyes are upon you." He instructs the singers to praise (praise will always bring about your victory) and God does something amazing as a result of their praise. The Lord sends ambushments against the enemy and in their confusion, the armies kill one another. If you read on to the end of chapter 20, you will see that the Lord caused them to win victoriously over their enemies and their test was turned into a triumph. If we can learn to look to the Lord and hear His Word, we will be assured of the same outcome that King Jehoshaphat received and our battle will turn into a blessing. Interestingly, the place where this tremendous victory happened was called The Valley of Berachah (vs 26). Berachah means "blessings" in Hebrew. When the Spirit of the Lord breathes courage into us as He did to Jeshoshaphat, He will turn our battles into blessings if we will praise Him!

These are just two of many incidents in Scripture when a person's outlook changed dramatically when the Spirit of the Lord visited their lives.

Let me remind you that this ability to see Him greater and mightier than the forces of wickedness that are out to destroy you does not come from positive thinking and is not the result of human will power. It comes from the Lord! It is divinely imparted to you when His Spirit breathes into you. It's part of our inheritance as the children of Abraham: the Blessing of Abraham. When that happens, you not only see things differently, you start to speak differently also!

Number 2. They Speak Differently!

Most of us are very familiar with the account of the Holy Spirit being poured out on the believers that assembled in the Upper Room in Acts 2:4. However, I would like to draw your attention to a less familiar verse that follows, Acts 2:11. "Cretes and Arabians, we do hear them speak in our tongues … the wonderful works of God."

Characteristically, those who have had an encounter with the Spirit of the Lord, those who have been breathed on by His Spirit, begin to speak "the wonderful works of God." Your speech changes when God's Spirit has come into your heart. On a personal note, every time I have had a glorious visitation in the Lord's presence, suddenly I have begun to speak prophetically and have begun to prophesy what He has shown me regarding my present circumstances and my future. I shared earlier in Chapter Two what happened on that fight to Mexico in January of 2003 and how as I started to speak what He had shown me, I began to see it come to reality in my life.

I remember that at first, I was a little apprehensive about sharing it with anyone because I was concerned about what they might think. I discovered this though; those that are truly your friends will celebrate your vision and what you believe the Lord has spoken to you, lending support and encouragement.

When God's Spirit has breathed into your heart and life, you speak the Word of the living God and His Word, which cannot return void (Isa. 55:11) activates things in the heavenlies and before long, they produce a result here on earth. God's Word is not like a boomerang that once it has been thrust from the thrower, returns back to him. No, His Word is like a divine arrow that always reaches its target and the place of its assignment. It always accomplishes what He wants it to accomplish" (Isa. 55:11).

The Word or the Scriptures are "God-breathed". 2 Timothy 3:16 says, "Every Scripture is God-breathed [given by His inspiration] and profitable for instruction, for reproof and conviction of sin, for correction of error and discipline in obedience, (and) for training in righteousness [in holy living, in conformity to God's will in thought, purpose, and action]. That is why we need to live in the Word daily. The Word of God is to our spirit-man what oxygen is to our physical man. Just as our bodies are dependent on it for life, so we are dependent on the God-breathed Word of God to sustain our spiritual life. Every time we read the Word and when I say read, I don't just mean skim over it or read it with our understanding and mentally, but when it is made a live to us by the Holy Spirit, it brings a quickening or a making alive to our inner man. Proverbs 4:22, speaking of the Word of God says, "It is life and health to all their flesh." One actually receives health and life from the Word because it is God-breathed, it breathes life and health into our beings and we are made whole by it. This too, is part of the blessing of Abraham.

Kings And Priests

I must credit Joseph Prince for helping to remind me of a truth in the Word of God that I have not only known but practiced for many years! Did you know that we who are believers in Christ actually have double-speaking power? Double-speaking power ... what does that mean? Revelation 1:5-6 says, "...unto Him that loved us and washed us from our sins in His own blood, and hath made us kings and priests unto God and his Father." Did you catch that? He is saying very clearly that you and I as believers are both "kings and priests" under the King of Kings and our High Priest, Jesus, our Lord and Savior. If that is the case, then we also have the same capacity that kings and priests have to speak and our words have power to make things happen. When a king speaks, or gives an edict for instance, his word is absolute, final and must be obeyed, or else. Ecclesiastes 8:4 says, "Where the word of king is, there is power." If the words of a king are powerful, then you and I as kings have power in our words. Words are powerful; they either speak life or death … blessing or cursing … prosperity or poverty and so on. It's important to make sure that what is coming out of your mouth aligns with what the King of Kings has said in His Word to us. Too often, the words that we speak seem almost contrary to what we know to be the Truth of God's word. I challenge you to weigh your words and make sure that they are in agreement with what He says about you and your situation and I promise you, you will begin to see some amazing things happen in your life.

As a king under the King of Kings, we must use the power of our words to speak authoritatively against the enemy and to speak life to our situations. There are times when you are in God's presence that you will sense the Word of the Lord become very real to you … a word of faith that quickens you and becomes alive in your spirit man. That's the time to speak it out of your mouth. The Word says we are "kings and priests." Did you know that in the Old Testament the office of a priest was not just a spiritual position, but he also held authority and power to settle matters of dispute with regard to property ownership, business matters and so on? If there was a contention over the value of an object, they would bring it before the priest and the priest would access a value to it; whatever the priest accessed the value to be, it was. In other words, the priest's words were authoritative and powerful. Deuteronomy 21:5 says, "Then the priests, the sons of Levi, shall come near, for the Lord your God has chosen them to serve Him and to bless in the name of the Lord; and every dispute and every assault [controversy] shall be settled by them." The priest's word was the final say in settling matters of controversy and conflict among the people; whatever the priest said, they had to accept and abide by. So, you and I, as priests under our High Priest, Jesus, have the authority to settle matters and speak peace to situations that won't seem to be settled any other way.

Enough Is Enough!

Allow me to share a personal testimony here. Several years back I was dealing with a matter that no matter how I prayed and even fasted about it, nothing would budge and it seemed as if I was at an impasse. It had gone on for a number of years and I had become quite frustrated about it until one day I was made aware of my double-speaking power and decided "enough was enough!" It was time to take authority over this problem and access and declare it "settled" because I had the authority to do so as a priest. To my amazement, several days later after speaking it settled in the Name of Jesus, the situation turned around completely and that began a healing process in the matter. Today, I look back and can pinpoint the turn around to that very day I spoke in authority over it and declared it "settled." Do you have a situation in your family, your marriage, your business, your finances or perhaps your ministry that refuses to yield and change? If you will use your double-speaking power as a king and a priest of the most High God, I promise you that thing will bow to the authority you have in Christ and you will start to see it change.

Speaking The Truth In Love

When The Blessing of Abraham is on your life, the words you speak are both Truth and Grace. Ephesians 4:15 says, "But speaking the truth in love, may grow up in all things into Him who is the head, Christ." You've probably heard someone say, "Well, I just tell it like it is and let the chips fall where they may." Or "I'm sorry, but the truth is the truth and I won't sugarcoat it." Well, speaking the truth is very important, but how you speak the truth is also important.

I heard noted Marriage Today speaker Jimmy Evans say, "Truth without love can be harsh, cutting, and even mean or cruel." That is why it's important to "speak the truth in love" or as Colossians 4:6 puts it, "Let your speech be always with grace, seasoned with salt, that you may know how you ought to answer each one." Grace takes the sting out of what can be the harshness of the truth. Grace makes it more palatable and easier to swallow. On the other hand, grace without truth is meaningless! It masks true feelings. Hiding and secrecy can be deadly, especially in a marriage relationship. Adam and Eve hid when they sinned and realized their nakedness. When God's Spirit is in your life, we can bring all things into the light of His love and then apply grace and love, which will heal the situation, relieve the tension and cause the anger to dissipate.

Did you know that the Lord watches to see that His Word is carried out? Jeremiah 1:12 says, "Then said the Lord to me, You have seen well, for I am alert and active, watching over My word to perform it" (AMP). This was one of my dear Mom's favorite scriptures that she gave me when I was going through a very tough time while in Bible College. The Lord was saying to the prophet Jeremiah, and prophetically to us, that it is important to SEE things the way God sees them and speak them accordingly; He will take care of the rest and fulfill His Word!

Number 3. They Think and Act Differently!

I believe that when the blessing of Abraham is on your life, you think and act differently than the rest. Just like was said of Caleb, he had another (different) spirit, so it is the case with those of us who are Spirit-filled believers today! When your mind has been renewed by God's Spirit, you now have the mind of Christ which is not limited to the constraints of the human mind. How a person thinks subsequently effects how that person acts. If you think you will never be a success or you will never get any breaks in life, that is essentially what you will experience. If we want to live overcoming, positive and productive lives and experience the full measure of God's abundant life and favor, we must make sure that our thoughts line up with what His Word declares. I realize that this is sometimes hard to do; believe me, I have struggled with my share of negative thinking throughout my walk with the Lord also, so I'm not casting judgment on anyone who may face some of the same kinds of struggles.

However, I have discovered that when I have had those special times in God's presence and His Spirit has visited my heart in a real and powerful way, that as a result of those encounters, my thinking became super-charged by the Holy Spirit and suddenly creative ideas started coming to my mind … solutions to problems, vision and optimism flooded my heart and once again I was filled with faith, believing that God has good plans for a prosperous future for me (Jer. 29:11). In particular, this was my experience back at the beginning of January 2010.

Just Before The Victory

As I mentioned, this was a very difficult time in some ways because everything that I had trusted in was suddenly gone and I was thrust into a new season by God's Spirit. I will admit, while I had some glorious times in prayer, at other times, I battled with feelings of defeat and negativity and the wicked one whispered thoughts like, "It's all over for you; you're finished," etc. If I had continued to entertain those thoughts I would have succumbed to the enemy's plan and thwarted God's awesome plans. Only the Lord knows where I would be today! I knew that the only way up was to get into the Word of God and let it breathe hope, faith and vision into my heart and renew my mind as He had done so many other times in my life at critical junctures, and that's exactly what I did.

God is my witness, all of a sudden, I began to see what God had in store for me and I began to get excited about it. "Coincidentally," I started getting international invitations to come and speak and doors began to open for me that I would never have dreamed of prior to that. I remember in March of 2010, I was preaching in Porto Alegre, Brazil for a wonderful man of God who pastors a great church there. After the Sunday a.m. service and after having had a great meal at a Churrascaria Restaurant (Brazilian style restaurant where they bring large skewers of various cuts of beef and other meats), they brought me back to my hotel room to rest before the evening service. I was tired, having preached and ministered several times already, so I really wanted to just sleep for an hour or so.

An Unexpected Visitation

The moment I laid my head on the pillow, suddenly, the names of countries started running through my mind. Then I heard the Spirit of the Lord say to me, begin to speak them out of your mouth ... South Africa, Columbia, Trinidad, Canada, and many more! I had heard Him say, "Every one of these that you speak out of your mouth, you will be going to and I will use you mightily for My glory." It was an awesome experience!

That night, after I had preached and ministered for hours, and the glory of the Lord had filled that church, the pastor, who is an Apostle of God, began to prophecy over me. Wouldn't you know, through the interpreter I heard him begin to call out the very same nations that I had spoken out of my mouth as I lay there in God's presence a few hours earlier. Wow! What a confirmation it was to my Spirit and I can testify to you today, five years later, I have been invited to and traveled to all of the above mentioned countries and seen the power of God in demonstration in each of them. Praise the wonderful Name of the Lord!

Why am I sharing this with you? Because if God's Spirit breathed on me and quickened my thinking, elevating my faith to believe, He can do it for you as well!

I discovered also, that after that experience in God's presence I began to act differently as well. I don't mean with arrogance or in a prideful manner, but rather a godly confidence came to my spirit and I carried myself differently than before. It affected my self esteem also and whereas I used to put myself down and think things like "I will never attain to the level of this preacher or that preacher" or "these kind of things only happen to the 'greats' of the Christian world, not me" ... this kind of thinking suddenly vanished. When I began to think of myself differently, I began to act differently and my reality soon matched what I was thinking.

I also had to shut out and separate myself from those who were not at a place to believe with me. As harsh as that may seem, sometimes, as well-meaning or well-intentioned as family and friends may be, they will hold you back from what God has prepared for you if their faith is limited or their vision for you is blinded by their preconceived ideas of you. Undoubtedly, that's why the Lord told our father Abraham to "get out your country" because He knew that Abraham's faith would have been effected by them!

I remember thinking that people saw me in a certain light ... as the choir director and worship leader for Pastor Benny ... and they probably would never see that there was more inside me and more that God wanted to do through my ministry. I had to leave that to God though and realize that if He could change my perception and my thoughts about myself, He could also change others as well. Sure enough, that has happened over the past five years and even Pastor Benny, who at one time, only saw me as his Music Director, now has referred to me as a wonderful preacher. I share that not to bring any glory to myself but to illustrate how obedience to God's timing brings promotion and blessing in your life. I hope this will encourage others in ministry who may feel like God has more for you but there just seems to be no outlet for the gifts He's placed inside of you or for expression of those gifts.

Prior to my encounter in 2003 when the Lord began to show me what He had in store for me, I couldn't imagine preaching under a heavy anointing as I have in the last five plus years. I could never have imagined being used by God's Spirit in the Word of Knowledge and Prophecy, or being used to lay hands on the sick and have them be instantly healed by the power of God ... but God did and it has been glorious! It took spending time in His presence for Him to breathe into my Spirit His plans for me and the ability to perform them.

The Unopened Gift

Wouldn't it be tragic if one day when you stand before the Lord, He begins to tell you, "I had this for you" or "I wanted to use you in this way, but you never allowed me to show you and therefore you forfeited them." I call it the tragedy of the unopened gift. Imagine if your husband or wife or some other loved one gave you a gift wrapped beautifully and after you thanked them for it, you put it on a shelf and never opened it. You would never know what that person had intended for you and you would never experience the blessing of that gift.

I believe that there are many in the body of Christ who are just like that. They've never truly received the gifts that God has given them and have thereby forfeited His divine intention for them. Spending time in His presence will unwrap the gift and reveal to you the heart and plans of the Savior for you. It will unlock the door to your destiny and usher you into a new season where God's miraculous power will be a reality.

In 2 Kings 6:1, the sons of the prophets realized that God had more for them and wanted to enlarge their territory and bring them into the fullness of His plan for them. "And the sons of the prophets said to Elisha, 'See now, the place where we dwell with you is too small for us'" (NKJV). The King James version says, "The place where we dwell with thee is too straight" (2 Kings 6:1).

What were they saying to the prophet Elisha? I believe they were saying, "As much as we enjoy your presence, as thrilling as it has been to see the power of God manifested through you, we are feeling like our own gifts are limited and there's no room for them to operate." God had put in them a desire for more … a desire to be used themselves in the same way. The only way that would happen was if they went to another place, a place where they had freedom to exercise their gifts and to see God use them just as he had their mentor, Elisha.

I'm not advocating that every Associate Pastor or Minister or whatever your subordinate roll or position may be in ministry, become dissatisfied and restless and hop from one position to the next instead of blooming where you're planted. However, if you've had an experience like the sons of the prophet did, and like I did where you realized that as much as you enjoyed your job, your friends and co-workers, that God had more for you and it will never happen because the place is too straight or limited, then get into God's presence and He will bring it about! Psalm 107:3 says, "Then they are glad because they are quiet; So He guides them to their desired haven."

God has a way of bringing about His plans and fulfilling the desires that He has placed in your heart. When He does, you will be glad and know that it was definitely Him who made it happen!

I encourage you to believe that like Caleb, you have another Spirit ... the Spirit of the Lord living and breathing in you ... and when you do, you will begin to see differently, speak differently, think differently and act differently! You will enter a new season in your life and begin to realize all of what God has planned for you.

The Blessing of a Heart Transplant and the Promise of Ezekiel 36

Have you ever known someone personally who has needed an organ transplant? Up until about a year ago, I had not. However, I recently made contact with a childhood friend of mine named Jackie whom I went to Sunday School, Youth Group and Church with in Nutley, New Jersey in my youth. Several years back, Jackie's kidneys became diseased and degenerated to the point that she was barely surviving with only 5% kidney function. Miraculously, Jackie continued to work a full time job, mainly because of great faith in the Lord to help her through each day, but in general, her quality of life was greatly diminished, and it had become apparent that without a transplant soon, the prognosis for her was bleak and she would most likely not live for more than a few months.

I was in Phoenix for ministry earlier this year and happened to have a couple hours of free time, so I paid a visit to Jackie and her Mom who have lived there for many years. Making a long story short, after some time of visiting and catching up on the years that have transpired, I felt led to pray for Jackie, laying hands on her as the scripture instructs us to do. Her Mom, Marie, a wonderful saint of the Lord who is very special to me and my family, joined in a prayer of agreement and we began to pray both in English and in tongues as the Holy Spirit prayed through us. I sensed the anointing in a powerful way and when we parted, I had an assurance in my heart that something had happened and that the Holy Spirit had begun a work of healing in Jackie's body.

Several days later, after having been through many disappointments of donor non-matches because of the anti-bodies in Jackie's diseased organ overpowering the antibodies of the prospective donor's antibodies making a transplant not possible, a call came from the Mayo Clinic and Jackie was told a suitable donor had been located. Jackie immediately responded and I am happy to report, the operation was a success, the transplanted kidney has been accepted by her body, and she has been restored to normal kidney function and her health is greatly improved over what it was just a few short months ago.

I can't help but believe that although Jackie owes a debt of gratitude to the donor, the amazing doctors and nurses who performed the transplant surgery and to the medical profession in general, that the Holy Spirit breathed on Jackie when we agreed in prayer and accelerated the process of matching her with a compatible donor. He ultimately is the One who has given her a new kidney and is healing her body. It's amazing how just one new organ can affect the health of the whole body!

I mention this story at this point to draw an analogy that if our entire body and health can be jeopardized by one malfunctioning organ, so our entire spiritual life can be affected by a diseased or deadened heart spiritually. The only remedy is a "transplant" by the Spirit of the Lord.

What do you mean by that, Jim? If we are being honest, we all go through times in our walk with the Lord when our hearts grow cold and somewhat hardened to the things of God because of letting the stuff of every day life crowd the Lord out. It's not necessarily intentional but it just happens because of the demands of every day life. It has been called the "tyranny of the urgent" where we are pulled in many directions between the needs of our spouse, parenting, household duties, job responsibilities, job stress, paying the bills, not having enough money to pay the bills, and on and on it goes. These things, along with the convenience that modern technology has provided such as our smart phones, iPads, and email, along with social media such as Facebook, Twitter and a host of others have resulted in an "always on" mode of life. Before you know it and without even realizing it, you find yourself just going through the motions, oblivious to the voice of God's Spirit with a heart that is in a hardened state. Worse yet, maybe we have allowed sinful habits and carnal things to take root in our hearts and like weeds in a garden, they have choked out the life of the good planting of the Lord. Now you find yourself in that epic battle between the appetites of the flesh and the desire to live godly in Christ Jesus but more often than not, you succumb to the dictates of the flesh which brings guilt, condemnation and shame.

How can one truly win in this battle and is it really possible to live an overcoming life? Even the Apostle Paul, a pillar of righteousness and a giant in the faith, admittedly struggled with this for he states the following in Romans 7:15-25:

"I do not understand what I do. For what I want to do I do not do, but what I hate I do. 16 And if I do what I do not want to do, I agree that the law is good. 17 As it is, it is no longer I myself who do it, but it is sin living in me. 18 For I know that good itself does not dwell in me, that is, in my sinful nature. For I have the desire to do what is good, but I cannot carry it out. 19 For I do not do the good I want to do, but the evil I do not want to do — this I keep on doing. 20 Now if I do what I do not want to do, it is no longer I who do it, but it is sin living in me that does it. 21 So I find this law at work: Although I want to do good, evil is right there with me. 22 For in my inner being I delight in God's law; 23 but I see another law at work in me, waging war against the law of my mind and making me a prisoner of the law of sin at work within me. 24 What a wretched man I am! Who will rescue me from this body that is subject to death? 25 Thanks be to God, who delivers me through

Jesus Christ our Lord! So then, I myself in my mind am a slave to God's law, but in my sinful nature a slave to the law of sin."

The Apostle Paul comes to the conclusion that the only way to win is "through Jesus Christ our Lord" who lives inside of us by His Spirit. Just like Ezekiel's prophecy to Israel centuries ago, it takes the breath of God to breathe into our "dry bones," giving us life and power over sin and the sinful nature.

You see the words spoken by Ezekiel in chapters 36 and 37 were given during a time when the Israelites were in captivity in a strange land, the result of their backsliding and turning from their God and worshipping pagan gods and living in immorality and utter neglect of God's righteous standards. Isn't it interesting that in the attempt of many to be free of rules and the "do's and don't's" of what they refer to as "religion," they wind up being enslaved to corrupt habits of a godless, sinful nature and not really free at all, all the while running from a "relationship" with God that can truly bring the freedom they are seeking after? But just like with His dealings with Israel, God, despite the state of our hardened hearts and open rebellion against Him and His laws, is showing us His mercy, compassion and willingness to restore us. Isn't that just like our God? How often we disregard His voice and in complete rebellion, disobey Him, yet His mercy endures and his grace towards us is inexhaustible. What a Savior!

A New Heart

Just as in the case where a human heart organ becomes so diseased and weakened to the point that it can no longer pump enough blood to the other parts of the body and the only remedy is a heart transplant operation, so it is in the spiritual realm. When the heart becomes so compromised by sin and rebellion or hardened because of neglect to God's Word or lack of breath, the only option is a total heart transplant by the Spirit of the Lord! This is exactly what the prophet is promising to Israel.

The prophet Ezekiel promises in Ezekiel 36:26-27: "A NEW heart also will I give you and a NEW Spirit will I put within you; and I will take away the stony heart out of you, and I will give you a heart of flesh." If you continue reading the rest of chapter 36 and then chapter 37 of Ezekiel, you see *how* a spiritual heart transplant happens; it happens by the breath of God!

Are you frustrated with your inability to completely obey the Lord's righteous standards, even though it is your heart to do so? There's good news! Ezekiel promises that when God breathes a new heart and a new Spirit into you, He gives that heart strength to overcome sin and live a life that is victorious over the flesh!

Ezekiel 36:27 says, "And I will put my Spirit within you, and *cause* you to walk in my statutes, and you will keep my judgments, and do them."

This promise to Israel was a foreshadowing of what happens when Christ's Spirit lives inside us. HE *causes* or makes us victorious over the flesh and helps us to be obedient to His Will. Praise God! The power to overcome is the direct result of God's Spirit breathing in you and empowering you to live godly in Christ Jesus just as He overcame when He walked here on earth.

He always brings revelation to our hearts and we now cannot only see what we are up against in spiritual warfare, but also gives us divine strategy and power to overcome the plans of the enemy.

One of the most profound and glorious aspects of the blessing of Abraham or the reviving breath of the Spirit of God in our lives is spiritual insight or revelation. The Apostle Paul put it this way: "the eyes of your understanding" in Ephesians 1:18, "will be enlarged." The Spirit of the Lord enables you to see things in the heavenly realm that you cannot see with the natural eye.

Supernatural Sight By The Spirit

Do you remember the familiar New Testament Bible story about the two men on the road to Emmaus? It's found in the gospel of Luke, chapter 24. The context of the story in the chapter is set immediately after the resurrection of Jesus from the dead. The two men, one of them being, Cleopas, the father-in-law of Matthew, the disciple and another not named man, were walking on their way to the village of Emmaus just outside of Jerusalem proper. (I have had the privilege to walk that very same road on my trips to the Holy Land, and it helped me envision this account with greater understanding.) As they are walking, they are talking about the Lord, and the fact that it is being heard about town, that He actually had raised from the dead, just as He said He would. At a certain point along their journey, a "Man" joins them and begins to walk with them, listening to their conversation. The Bible tells us in verse 16, "But they were kept from recognizing Him" (NIV). Without the Spirit of the Lord, our eyes are kept from recognizing (seeing) Him and the things of His Supernatural Kingdom. So, He (the Lord, the man who joined them) asks them in verse 17, "What are you discussing as you walk together?"

Cleopas responds to His question a bit sarcastically in verse 18 of the same chapter, saying, "Are you the only one in Jerusalem who does not know of the things that have happened there?" The Lord responds, "What things?" He is speaking as if He doesn't know since it's obvious that they do not recognize Him yet. In the following verses, they begin to expound to Him about Jesus, starting with His coming from Nazareth, being a mighty prophet of the Word and miracles to the people. They go on to say how the chief priests and rulers apprehended Him, condemned Him to death, and crucified Him. They had trusted He would be the Redeemer of Israel and this is the third day since He had been put to death. In fact, certain women of their company were astonished when they visited His tomb because His body was missing and had seen a vision of angels which said, "He is alive!" This had been verified by others of their company who went to check it out themselves and found it to be as the women had said.

Jesus rebukes them, calling them "fools" and "slow to believe" (vs 25). Beginning with Moses and all the prophets He expounds to them the scriptures and things concerning Himself. Remember, they still do not have a clue as to who this man is that is now speaking so passionately to them. What happens next is why I am including this story here because it illustrates perfectly my point that an encounter with the Lord of glory brings spiritual revelation and heavenly perception.

Fellowship And Communion

Verse 28 tells us that as they are getting closer to the village of Emmaus, this stranger makes as though He was would go on further down the road and pass the entrance to the village of Emmaus. But what happens next is a profound key to what is required for us, even today, to bring vision and divine revelation to our spiritual eyes. Verse 29 says, "They constrained Him" (KJV) or in the NIV translation, "They urged Him strongly" Stay with us, for it is nearly evening; the day is almost over." So he went in to stay with them."

If your desire is to see things the way God sees them and to experience Ephesians 1:18 … "the eyes of your understanding being opened," … then it is necessary to learn how to "constrain Him" or "urge Him strongly" to come to your house and spend time with Him in fellowship and communion. In our modern day, constraining Him or urging Him strongly to visit us might require disconnecting from technological conveniences like our smart phones, the internet, our iPads or whatever may be demanding our attention for a while so that we can communicate with Him in prayer so He can speak to us and reveal Himself to us. The passage in Luke 24:30-31 goes on to tell us that the reward for urging Him to stay, to come to their house and eat with them, was that their blindness left them. "When He was at the table, He took bread, gave thanks, and broke it and began to give it to them." (vs 30) and immediately after He did that, "their eyes were opened and they recognized Him, and He disappeared from them" (vs 31).

If we invite Him to come to our house, He will respond and not only will He "break bread" with us but in that divine exchange, He will open the eyes of our understanding and reveal Himself to us. This is what we do when we celebrate the communion in our services. It's not just a ritual to be done out of obligation, but rather an opportunity to truly commune with Him and have our hearts and bodies quickened (made alive) by His Holy Spirit, renewing us in body, mind and spirit. It is also an opportunity for fresh revelation of the Savior and also a revelation of who we are in Him.

It is in these moments, that we experience a heart transplant spiritually and we begin again to experience the joy of our salvation. There is no problem too difficult or no degree of decay that cannot be brought back to life by the breath of God's Spirit breathing on it!

If you have been experiencing any of what I have just been describing, I encourage you to stop right here as you are reading and pray this prayer with me:

"Holy Spirit, I recognize my need for Your quickening, healing and restoring breath in my heart and life. I ask You now to breathe upon my deadness, my emptiness, my dryness and the hardness of my heart and my rebellion against your righteous ways, and touch me once again with Your renewing Spirit as You have promised. Give me a New Heart and a New Spirit; one that delights in You and in Your ways; take away the stony heart and replace it with Your heart of flesh. Amen!"

My Prayer

After a time of fasting and prayer back in the early 90's, I woke up one morning with this song titled "Fill This Temple," which has now been sung around the world. The lyrics are really a prayer from the heart that the Holy Spirit will respond to:

"Let my heart be the Temple of Your Spirit
Let my spirit feel the warmth of Your embrace.
Let me be a holy habitation,
Where Your Spirit is pleased to dwell
Oh Lord, I long to know Your glory
I want to offer the sacrifice of praise
Fill this temple, Lord, with Your Spirit once again."
– words and music by Jim Cernero

This prayer in song came out of a deep yearning in my heart to know Him and His glory in a way that I had not yet previously known Him. To this day, there is an anointing on the chorus and when it is sung, the presence of the Lord becomes very real to all who are present worshipping.

I can say with confidence that if you prayed that prayer earnestly, the Holy Spirit has heard you and He has already begun to breathe into your spirit.

The Heart of The Matter

Statistical evidence of "emotional heart problems" in relationships appears to be on the increase in every area of society. With the divorce rate among Christian couples rising to almost the same level as non-Christian marriages, I maintain that the root cause of many marital breakups is this need for a heart transplant. Remember how it was when you first fell in love with you husband or your wife? You were on cloud nine, as they say, and everything he or she did or said made your heart warm and respond accordingly. But perhaps along the way, a wall may have begun to come between you because of hurts and unresolved conflict, and before you know it, the heart becomes indifferent to the one who is the perceived inflictor. Now the couple is living in an emotional divorce although they may stay together for the sake of the children or for appearance sake.

When this stage of indifference sets in, as well-intentioned as a word or a gesture may be, nothing that the other partner does is perceived in the manner to which it is said or done because it is filtered through a prism or discolored lens which distorts, twists and only piles on to the hurt. Only the Holy Spirit can begin to chip away at that wall and begin to break it down. That will only happen when He breathes into both the hearts involved and gives a new heart and a new spirit in place of the hardened, embittered and closed off heart that has developed. I have seen this miracle take place in my own family members so I speak with first hand experience that God can and will restore and will take away the stony heart and give a heart of flesh (a healed, non-diseased heart) in its place if both are willing to let Him do so.

Established In Him By Him

You see, the presence of the Lord is a stabilizing factor in a marriage. Colossians 17 says, "And is before all things and by Him all things consist." If you look up the word "consist" in the original Greek, you find that it means "are held together." When Christ is the central figure in a marriage or in our lives in general, He "holds things together" and keeps us from falling apart. When I perform marriage ceremonies, I use the example of a 3-fold cord. Two strands of rope have a certain degree of strength. However, if you wrap those two cords around a center cord, the strength of the rope becomes exponentially stronger and is much less likely to unravel or break apart! That is exactly how it is when Christ is the "center cord" or the central figure in a marriage. He provides a strength that is much greater than the sum of just the two. He will hold you together through the rough passes and challenges that all marriages go through. As we bring our spouse and the situation to Him in prayer, He will breathe new life into the deadness and bleakness of the situation and turn it around for His glory.

Maybe as you're reading this book your marriage is struggling like I have just described above. Let me encourage you with this fact: the Lord knows how to fix the situation and He is able to do miracles despite what may seem hopeless right now. Ask the Holy Spirit to breathe His life-giving breath into your heart and into your marriage. To give you a NEW heart; to give your spouse a new heart also … one that's sensitive to His voice, pliable and open to His leading … and He will fulfill Ezekiel 36:26-27 in your life and in those that you love and give you a heart transplant. Amen.

The prophet Ezekiel continues his prophecy from chapter 36 and shows how it will be fulfilled in the children of Israel in the following chapter, chapter 37 of Ezekiel. He describes Israel's state in a much worse condition than even he did in chapter 36. He likens it to a body that has not only died, but has decayed to the point that only a skeleton of dry bones remains. When all that is left is bones, it's pretty apparent that there's been a death! Maybe you feel like all that's left is "dry bones" and you are dead spiritually. Perhaps despite your prayers, your financial situation, your physical health, your relationships, your dreams and visions all seem to be dead and reminiscent of the scene described in Ezekiel 37, and you are asking, "Can these bones live?" (Ez. 37:3). Take heart, be encouraged! There's good news. The answer is YES! Ezekiel goes on to prophesy centuries ago, what is now being fulfilled in Israel and what can and will happen in our lives when God begins to breathe life into us.

Ezekiel 37:4-5 says, "Again He said to me, "Prophesy over these bones and say to them, 'O dry bones, hear the word of the Lord.' Thus says the Lord God to these bones, 'Behold, I will cause breath to enter you that you may come to life" (AMP). (The Blessing of Abraham or the "hey" of His Spirit.)

Ezekiel prophesies under the inspiration of God's Spirit and says that the dry bones will live. When God breathes in you, the Spirit of prophecy comes on you and you begin to speak prophetically about your outcome or your future. You speak life into the deadness of your situation … long before there is any sign of it happening in the natural. He goes on to prophesy over Israel's deadness. Ezekiel 37:7-8 declares, "So I prophesied as I was commanded; and as I prophesied, there was a noise, and behold a shaking, and the bones came together, bone to his bone. And when I beheld, lo, the sinews and the flesh came up upon them, and skin covered them above; but there was no breath in them" (KJV).

These verses show the fulfillment of Ezekiel's prophecy and what has been happening in the Holy Land since 1948 when it became a nation and many of the Jews who had been scattered around the world started returning to Israel. But although they have returned, many of them still have not had a revelation of Christ Jesus as their Messiah which is why the prophet said, "…but there was no breath in them."

Without Breath There Is No Life

A body can be completely in tact but without breath, it is still dead. This is the case with Israel today and is with those who don't know Jesus as their Lord and Savior and who have not been breathed in by the Holy Spirit … appearing to be whole, but none-the-less, dead because of no divine breath in them. However, when God breathes, everything changes and death is conquered by His breath of life just as will one day happen with Israel when they recognize the Lord as their Messiah.

Ezekiel 37:9-10 says, "Then said he unto me, Prophesy unto the wind, prophesy, son of man, and say to the wind, Thus saith the Lord God; Come from the four winds, O breath, and breathe upon these slain, that they may live. (vs 10) So I prophesied as he commanded me, and the breath came into them, and they lived and stood up upon their feet, an exceeding great army" (KJV).

The result of God's breath upon Israel will soon result in them coming to the awareness that the Messiah for whom they have been searching for centuries has indeed come and His Name is Yeshua ... Jesus! After this awakening will be a rising up as a great army to fight the great battle of Armegedon described in the book of Revelation. I have stood in the valley of Megiddo in Israel where this great apocalyptic battle will take place, and it is a sobering experience to realize what will one day take place there.

Sadly as, anti-semitism is once again unthinkably on the rise and the horror of the holocaust is becoming a fading memory for some, I believe that the Lord will use the church of Jesus Christ to befriend the Jewish people and show them the love of their true Messiah.

Just as will happen with Israel, God will breathe His restoring, life-giving, recreating breath into our deadness and our dry bones will live again. How does this happen? It happens when you and I have an encounter like Abraham did in Genesis 17:5 and the "hey" of the Spirit of the Lord breathes into us. It is the result of the Blessing of Abraham on our lives. It happens when we realize the truth of Galatians 3:14 which states "that the blessing of Abraham might come on the Gentiles; the promise of the Spirit through faith."

CHAPTER FIFTEEN

I Just Want Breath To Praise Him

One of my most cherished memories of my precious mother that has become a life lesson to me happened at a most unexpected time and in a most unusual setting. It is also a very fitting example of just what the blessing of Abraham can do in a life and demonstrates the truth that I have been declaring to you in this book.

In 2007, my precious, godly mother became seriously ill when three of the tiny arteries that supplied blood to the heart became blocked. We were informed that the doctors could not do open heart surgery due to her weakened condition nor traditional angioplasty (the balloon treatment that is inserted into the artery and as it expands, it opens up the artery allowing for better blood flow) due to the precarious location of the blocked arteries behind her heart. She had undergone open heart surgery twenty years earlier and for the most part, had been in relatively good health until this reoccurrence in 2007.

Soon she became so weak and breathless that she couldn't walk but just a few steps without having difficulty breathing or collapsing. I, along with two of my brothers, John and Mark, who are also ministers and also lived out of state from New Jersey where my Mom resided, were taking turns visiting as often as possible, despite the demands of our busy schedules. We visited on a rotating schedule to help our eldest brother, Tom, who lived in New Jersey and cared for Mom. It was so hard to see her in that state but despite what was happening in her body, her faith never wavered and she kept on declaring the Word of God that says in Exodus 15:26, "I Am the God that heals you," and Isaiah 53:5, "… with His stripes we are healed."

My Mom was a woman of the Word! She not only loved the Word but would pray the Word of God, speak the Word of God, and write the Word often. She would fill lined pads of paper with healing verses and the promises of God's Word. Having dealt with many health issues throughout her life, as I mentioned in an earlier chapter, she believed that God could use doctors and medical science. Above all, however, she knew that Jesus is the Great Physician and that the answer to health and healing is found in the Word of God. She had long ago discovered the truth of Proverbs 4:22 which says that the Word of God is "life and health to all their flesh."

Surprised By A Phone Call

It is interesting to note also that my Mom had an affinity for healing ministries and was a partner with several of the major ministries, perhaps because she, herself, had needed healing often. I can remember as a young boy attending an Oral Roberts tent meeting in Teaneck, New Jersey not far from where I grew up. I also recall going to Pittsburgh, Pennsylvania to be in a Kathryn Kuhlman service. Little did she know back then that one day, one of her own sons would be on staff and travel the world with one of the largest healing ministries, Benny Hinn Ministries!

It was my Mom, in fact, who introduced me to Pastor Benny's ministry. It was in the fall of 1987 when my wife and I stayed with her and my Dad for several weeks during a transitional season in our lives due to an unexpected turn of events, through no fault of our own that left me temporarily without a job. I remember her being enthused about this "Benny Hinn" who, up until then, I had never heard of. I will never forget the look on my Mom's face when just a few days into our stay with my parents, she answered the phone and on the other end of the line was Benny Hinn, whom she had been telling me about!

A day earlier, I had called a friend of mine, the well known gospel singer, John Hall (aka "Big John" because he's a tall Texan with a big bass voice) to ask him to keep me in mind if he happened to hear of a Music Minister/Worship Leader position opportunity as he traveled to many of the major Evangelical churches at that time. The Word says, "The steps of a righteous man are ordered of the Lord," and that call to John turned out to be quite providential and a divine connection for my life and ministry!

God's Amazing Timing

As it just so "happened," the very day that I called John, he was scheduled to be the music guest on the "Praise The Lord" program on TBN. The guest that evening was none other than Benny Hinn. John was scheduled to sing in the early part of the program that night and Pastor Benny was to speak later on the program. They met in the green room at TBN and greeted one another as they also knew each other well. Pastor Benny said to John, "John, don't leave afterward; I need to speak to you." John, who also enjoyed Pastor Benny's ministry, was more than happy to stay and obliged the request.

When the program ended and they met again in the green room, Pastor Benny said to John, "I'm looking for a Minister of Music/Worship Leader; do you know of one who is anointed and available?"

In his deep voice John said, "Why yes, as a matter of fact I do. His name is Jim Cernero."

Immediately Pastor Benny replied, "Who is this Jim Cernero, tell me about him." Then in typical Pastor Benny style, he said in then still quite noticeable accent, "Marvelous, let's call him right now, brother!" So they picked up the phone and called my Mom and Dad's house phone (this was before cell phones) and to her shock and amazement, when my Mom picked up the phone, she heard Pastor Benny's voice! After introducing himself and some kind words from my Mom telling him how much she enjoyed his ministry, he asked to speak to me. Of course, dear Mom, who was beaming from ear to ear, said, "Jim, dear, it's Benny Hinn!"

I was just as surprised as she was because at first, I couldn't imagine how he had found out about me or gotten my Mom's phone number. I wasn't aware that he and John Hall were friends, nor that John was even scheduled to see him at TBN ... but the Lord knew! We spoke briefly and the next thing I knew, he had invited me and my wife to Orlando for an interview. A few days later, we were on a plane headed to sunny Florida from New Jersey. That would be a pivotal turning point in our lives and ministry.

From that time on, my Mom grew to love Pastor Benny and Suzanne and would pray for them like she did her own children. They loved her too as often times down through the 22 years that I served his ministry full time, Mom and Dad when he was still alive, had attended Orlando Christian Center when visiting us in Orlando. They also attended a number of the crusades that were in the New Jersey, New York Metropolitan area.

Twenty Years Later

So now, in the spring of 2007 — 20 years after I began to work with Pastor Benny — she became deathly ill and was in need of a miracle once again, trusting the Lord who had been faithful to heal her many times before, to do it once again. At the time, my wife and I, along with our son, Daniel, were living in Orange County California, not far from Pastor Benny's Ministry Studio, which is located about an hour south of Los Angeles. Pastor Benny had scheduled an international crusade in Berlin, Germany and I remember boarding the plane in LAX airport on my way to Berlin with a heavy heart because of my Mom's deteriorating condition. Thankfully and providentially, my connection to the overseas flight was in JFK airport in New York City. As soon as the plane landed at JFK, I turned on my cell phone and called my twin brother, John, who was then visiting my Mom for an update on her condition. When I heard his voice, I could tell by his tone that things had gone from bad to worse and he said, "Jim, you'd better come now if you want to see her again here on earth." She had gone into complete heart failure and her lungs were filled with fluid because of the blockages. He said, "The doctors don't think she'll make it through the night."

Needless to say, my heart sank as I heard the news. I was faced with a dilemma: go on to Berlin for the crusade and pray that my Mom would survive this or go immediately to the hospital in Tom's River, New Jersey where my Mom lay in her hospital bed, possibly not making it through the night. I called Pastor Benny and explained the situation and how critical my Mom was. He was most gracious and said, "Jim, you only have one mother; go to her and we will figure out what to do in Berlin." After thanking him, I rented a car and drove the two hours down to the shore area of New Jersey from JFK Airport, praying and interceding for my Mom in the Spirit the entire way.

The Unforgettable Whispered Words

I arrived at the hospital very late in the evening, and I will never forget seeing my Mom laying there on the bed in ICU, struggling to breathe with no color in her face. My Mom was a woman of small stature — barely 5 feet tall — but a giant in the Spirit when it came to matters of faith. I leaned over the bed rail and said in a soft voice, "Mom, I'm here." Her eyes opened and she smiled and then she said something to me that I will never forget! With the little bit of breath she could gather to barely whisper she said, "Jim … I just want breath to praise Him." She could have said, I just want the Lord to heal me or take away the pain, but no, true to form, her one desire was to praise her precious Lord and Savior, Jesus whom she adored and served all the days of her life. You see, my Mom had discovered many years earlier that praise is a key to your victory, your healing, your answer; it defeats the enemy and releases the blessing of grace, the blessing of Abraham on your life.

Psalm 149:6 says, "Let the high praises of God be in their mouth and a two-edged sword in their hand." High praise or praise that happens when you've been in the high place, the presence of the Lord, cripples the power of the wicked one and brings about your victory. In response to Mom saying, "I just want breath to praise Him" I said, "The Lord will give you breath to praise Him, Mom," but truthfully, I didn't know if that would be here on earth or when she got to heaven.

I stayed with her for a short while longer, praying with her, holding her hand and telling her that I loved her and that many were praying for her healing (she loved hearing that) and then I walked towards the door of the hospital room to let her rest and try to get some sleep for the night.

Prompted By The Holy Spirit

As I got to the door, I heard the Holy Spirit speak to my spirit, "Go get your iPod." He reminded me that on my iPod, I had a recording of healing scriptures that Pastor Benny had done several months before. On it he reads healing verses from Genesis to Revelation while myself and Sheryl Palmquist, who played keyboards and the organ for the crusades for many years, played appropriate healing choruses and songs as background music to the scripture reading CD. It's not a highly produced recording but it's anointed because the Word is anointed and the Word is God-breathed. Many have been healed just listening to it because as I have said before, the Word of God is "life and health to their flesh" (Prov. 4:22). I walked back to Mom and asked, "Would you like me to get my iPod with the healing scriptures on it so you can listen to it while you lay here and fall asleep?" She said in a whispered voice, "Oh yes, that would be wonderful, Jim!" Remember, I told you that my Mom loved the Word of God and loved to write it, but now she was too weak to even sit up or hold a pen to write.

I ran to the car, opened my brief case and found the iPod. When I got back to the room, I put the earphones in her ears and adjusted the volume to a low, comfortable level so that all night long she could hear the Word as she lay there in that hospital bed. When

I kissed her again and said good-bye, I honestly didn't know if I would ever see her alive here on earth again. All through the night in that hospital room in Toms River, New Jersey, as that recording of healing scriptures played in my Mom's ears, the Spirit of the Lord was breathing (the Blessing of Abraham) life into her nearly dead body and what happened a few hours later was truly and without a doubt in my mind, a miracle!

A New Day

In the morning, my brothers and I were eager to get a report on Mom's condition so I called the hospital and the receptionist transferred the call to the nurses' station in ICU where my Mom was. When I got through to the nurse I said, "This is Jim Cernero, Rachel Cernero's son. Could you give me a report on how my Mom is doing today? The nurse replied, "Just a second." The way she said, "Just a second" caught my attention! I didn't know whether to be worried or if she was just busy at the moment.

While waiting for her to come back to the phone, I remember thinking, "The computer with my Mom's chart is right there in front of her at the nurses' station desk; why didn't she just read it and give me a report?" The next thing I heard as God is my witness that I'm telling you the truth, was my Mom's voice, not weak, not breathless like a few hours earlier, but strong. "Jim," she exclaimed. "The Lord touched me! I can breathe, I can praise Him!" I still get goose bumps thinking about it to this day! She was praising and thanking the Lord because He answered her prayer and gave her breath back to praise Him once again.

Do you know what it was, dear reader? It was the Blessing of Abraham! The Holy Spirit had breathed into her weakened body and had quickened (made alive) her failing heart and lungs by His Divine, healing power once again. The same Spirit that breathed the "hey" of His Spirit, that fifth letter of the Hebrew alphabet, the Spirit of Grace into Abraham and Sarah and quickened their bodies ... that same Spirit that raised Jesus from the dead ... had now breathed into His servant Rachel Cernero His life-giving breath, healing her as she lay there in His presence and the Word touched her and made her whole! Hallelujah!

My description of my Mom's condition is completely without exaggeration so the miracle that I have just shared with you was really quite remarkable! She went from barely being able to walk a few steps and struggling to breathe, to being able to once again do light housework, cooking and even traveling to her grandsons' weddings by plane. I pray that this has stirred your faith to believe that God's Holy Spirit can and will do the same in your situation if you believe and ask Him to.

The Glory of God Revealed

The morning after she was healed, when the nurse who had been attending my Mom throughout this entire ordeal entered the room, she gasped and said, "Mrs. Cernero! There's an aura about you!" My Mom, never missing an opportunity to witness for the Lord said, "Oh no, dear...what you're seeing is the glory of God because He touched me last night!"

When the Spirit of the Lord visits your heart and life, it is sometimes noticeable to those around you. Moses' face shown with the radiance of God's glory (Ex. 34:29) when he came down off of Mt. Sinai and the children of Israel noticed it, so we shouldn't be surprised if the glory of God can be seen on us as well.

Although she is now with the Lord in glory, my Mom lived for another seven years until 87 years of age. Each day, she would sit at her piano and play worship choruses and many of her favorite hymns in praise to Jesus, Lord and Savior, who had many times been her Healer as well! She even attended one more Benny Hinn crusade in New Jersey. During that crusade Pastor Benny had her come to the platform to testify of her healing and sing her favorite hymn, "Great is Thy Faithfulness." Mom had a lovely soprano voice and used it to sing praise to the Lord all her life. Pastor Benny later aired that part of the service on his program, "This is Your Day," and it was seen by thousands of people around the world.

At her funeral in May of 2013, we played a video tape of her playing the piano and the segment of her sharing her testimony and singing at a Benny Hinn Ministries crusade in New Jersey, and you could sense the presence of the Lord on the video.

I felt it appropriate to share this wonderful testimony of my Mom's healing in 2007 because of that amazing statement she said to me when I arrived at her hospital room … "I just want breath to praise Him." It still resonates within me and I believe it illustrates so perfectly what can and will happen if we realize that as part of "the blessing" it is ours as children of Abraham and as believers in Christ Jesus! We can experience the same miraculous power of God that breathed into Father Abraham and his wife Sarah if we will only believe and accept it by faith! Nothing is too difficult for God! Nothing that has been perpetrated by the hand of the wicked devil can withstand the awesome power of our mighty God!

"When I catch the first breath of the Spirit, I leave everything and everybody to be in His presence, to hear what He has to say to me." — Smith Wigglesworth, *The Secret Of His Power, p 53*

CHAPTER SIXTEEN

Receiving and Releasing the Blessing

Perhaps after reading all of this, you still question in your heart, "Is this really for me? After all Jim, I'm not a Jew by ethnicity; I'm a Christian. How do you know that this truth about the Blessing of Abraham applies to me or to Christians in general? Besides, isn't that essentially an Old Testament message? Aren't we New Testament believers?" Even if I understand the blessing and recognize how it benefited the individuals in the scriptural examples you've given us in this book, how do we receive the blessing? How do we as believers today use it? What are the steps or keys to activating this blessing of Abraham that you've been talking about in this book?

If any of these questions came to mind, I'm glad you asked! The reason I know that all that I have shared in the book is not only for the physical descendants of Abraham but is definitely yours and mine to claim and experience is because the Word of God says so and that's enough for me! Where, you ask? Of all places, in the NEW Testament! Even if you were inclined to dismiss it because it was OLD Testament, and therefore in your mind conclude it's not for us believers today because we are under the New dispensation of Grace, then listen to what the Apostle Paul wrote to the new testament church in Galatia in the book of Galatians, a New Testament book!

Galatians 3:6-7 says, "Just as Abraham 'believed God, and it was accounted to him for righteousness.' therefore know that only those who are of faith are sons of Abraham" (NKJV).

The First Step to Receiving the Blessing

Question: Are you of faith? By that I mean, have you believed on the Lord Jesus Christ, acknowledged your need of forgiveness from sin and accepted Him as your Savior? Then the fact is, the Bible says you are of faith and you are a child or son or daughter of Abraham. Those who have believed on Him and accepted Him by faith are part of the body of Christ. If you have answered this ultimate question and accepted Jesus Christ as your Lord and Savior, then, as a son or daughter of Abraham, the blessing of Abraham belongs to you too! This is the first and most important step to receiving the blessing of Abraham in your life.

If you cannot honestly answer this question, then I've got very good news for you as well. As I said in the chapter titled The Blessing of Salvation and Righteousness, the act of getting saved or salvation is really quite simple; it comes down to believing and confessing!

Once again, if you will pray this prayer with me now, I can assure you that after you do, you will be saved and you will be able to say and agree with the Apostle Paul that you are of faith and will qualify for the blessing.

Prayer:
Lord Jesus, I believe You are the Son of the Living God. I believe You came and died for my sins on the cross of Calvary. I ask You to forgive my sins and cleanse my heart. Make me a new creation in Your Son, Christ Jesus. Help me to live for You from this day on. I now confess You are my Lord, my Savior and I thank You that according to Your word, I am saved. Amen!"

If you just prayed that prayer with all your heart, you are now a Christian and are saved. You are also "of faith" according to the Word of God … a child of Abraham. That means all that was promised to Abraham's children, grandchildren and the generations that have followed belongs to you also! Welcome to the family! Now, receive the blessing of Abraham … your rightful inheritance in Christ.

If you prayed this prayer, please take time to email me at the following email address and let me know about your decision to invite Jesus to be the Lord and Savior of your life. info@certainsoundministries.org. I want to encourage you and help you grow in the knowledge of our Lord.

Whenever I preach this message, I ask the congregation the same question I asked you a little earlier in this chapter: "Are you of faith?" Most of the congregation will respond "yes." Then I go on to say, well, here's what the Word says about you. If you are of faith, "The same are the children of Abraham" (Gal. 3:7). That is very good news! That means that all that Abraham's children or descendants were /are in line to receive, you and I who are of faith, are also in direct line to receive! That means that everything that I have been talking about in this book, the same breath of the Spirit of God, that fifth letter of the Hebrew alphabet (hey) and all that goes along with it is yours today to experience by faith.

The Second Step to Receiving the Blessing

Now that you know that you are of faith and are born again by the Spirit of the Lord, have a knowledge of what belongs to you as a child of Abraham, it is important to "take" what is yours and begin to utilize it in your every day life! How do I do that, Jim? The first step to taking what is yours is to receive the Baptism of the Holy Spirit as mentioned in the book of Act, chapter two, verses two through four.

"And suddenly there came a sound from heaven as of a rushing mighty wind, and it filled all the house where they were sitting. 3 And there appeared unto them cloven tongues like as of fire, and it sat upon each of them. 4 And they were all filled with the Holy Ghost, and began to speak with other tongues, as the Spirit gave them utterance" (Acts. 2:2-4).

The moment I received the Baptism of the Holy Spirit in 1968, as I described to you in Chapter Six, The Blessing of Peace, my entire life changed and was altered by that encounter like Abraham of old. Prior to that, I was a somewhat timid and shy young boy but when the Spirit filled me, I discovered an ability to stand before people and share without fear and intimidation. I could never have imagined that God would ordain for that same previously timid young man, to stand before crowds as large as 1 million in Bangalore, India to lead worship and help bring the message of salvation and healing! That's what the power of the Spirit can do in a life!

A New Dimension of Power

The baptism of the Holy Spirit is the infilling and empowering of the Holy Spirit as referred to in Acts 2:4, which brought the followers of Christ into a new dimension of power … power to witness and testify of the Jesus Christ of Nazareth despite the constant threat of persecution and even death at the hands of the Romans. Peter, who had denied the Lord three times during Jesus' trial and crucifixion, suddenly becomes a mighty preacher and 3,000 are born again through his witness on the Day of Pentecost! He became "another man" when the Spirit came into his life. He now ministered with the anointing (power of God) and when he did, it produced amazing results. This glorious experience activates the blessing of Abraham or the promise of the Spirit in the life of a believer.

Not only did they have power to witness but they also had power to do miracles in the Name of Jesus!

Shortly after this heavenly outpouring of the Spirit, just as Jesus had promised, Peter and John are walking up to the temple and they encounter a man who had been lame from his mother's womb who would daily ask for alms from those who entered the temple. Acts. 3:4-10 gives us the account of what happened by the Holy Spirit's power.

"And fixing his eyes on him, with John, Peter said, "Look at us." 5 So he gave them his attention, expecting to receive something from them. 6 Then Peter said, "Silver and gold I do not have, but what I do have I give you: In the name of Jesus Christ of Nazareth, rise up and walk." 7 And he took him by the right hand and lifted him up, and immediately his feet and ankle bones received strength. 8 So he, leaping up, stood and walked and entered the temple with them—walking, leaping, and praising God. 9 And all the people saw him walking and praising God. 10 Then they knew that it was he who sat begging alms at the Beautiful Gate of the temple; and they were filled with wonder and amazement at what had happened to him" (NKJV).

An immediate after effect of the infilling of the Holy Spirit, the Baptism of the Holy Spirit brought a new authority to say, "Rise up and walk," and to perform this mighty miracle which was a testimony of the Lord's power and presence in them.

Throughout my life as a Spirit-filled believer, I have seen first hand the change that comes over a man or woman of God when the anointing of the Spirit comes on them and an authority to use the power of the Spirit to bring about miracles. My Grandfather, Thomas

Tarantino, as I mentioned in the chapter seven titled The Blessing of a Godly Heritage of Faith, was one of my earliest examples of this but certainly not the last. Obviously, I have watched Pastor Benny on platforms around the world when the anointing of the Spirit comes on him, and how within a matter of minutes, God is using him to bring healing to many in the audience. Now, I see it in myself as I minister with such anointing and authority that at times, I can almost step outside of myself and it's as if I'm watching another of myself working with the Holy Spirit. What an amazing God that He can use us in such a way and bring about miracles when we step out in faith and use the power He has given us!

You see, my friend, this experience is like the opening of a door that unlocks all of the aspects of the blessing that I have been talking about in this book. It's an encounter with the Spirit of Grace, the Holy Spirit, and from Him flows all of the benefits that I have attempted to describe to you such as salvation and righteousness, healing, peace, supernatural power to do the impossible, supernatural intervention, divine protection and more.

What about you, my friend? Have you had this wonderful experience since you became a believer? It's available to you and is a free gift to all who believe. In fact, you don't even have to be in a church service for the Lord to fill you and baptize you with His Spirit (the blessing of Abraham). He can fill you right now as you're reading this book! All you need to do is ask Him to. As happened in the above mentioned passage of scripture in Acts 2:4, He will fill you with His spirit and you will begin to speak with other tongues as the Holy Spirit gives you the words. This heavenly language will assist you in your prayer life and help you to pray in the Spirit and according to the will of God. It will transform you and give you power to become a witness for Christ and to step out in His authority and yes, even work miracles in Jesus' Name. Let me lead you in a prayer right now and expect Him to fill you as you pray.

Prayer:

"Holy Spirit, promised One from the Lord Jesus, third Person of the Trinity, breathe on me now as You did on the believers in the Upper Room on the Day of Pentecost and fill me with the Holy Ghost and power. I ask You to give me Your power to become a mighty witness for Your Kingdom and to work miracles as a sign to the unbeliever. Activate the blessing of Abraham in my life and release Your power in me and through me I pray! In the Name of the Father, the Son, and the Holy Spirit. Amen!"

If you prayed that prayer with sincerity, I know that the Lord Jesus, Who is the baptizer, has heard and will answer your prayer! Why not spend a few moments right now worshipping Him audibly and as you do, I believe you will receive the baptism of the Spirit and He will give you a new language with which to praise Him and with which to pray powerfully from this point on. As a minister of the gospel, I agree with you for it and believe that right now, many of you are being filled with the Spirit of God! Amen.

The Third Step Is a Personal Revelation of The Blessing

Need a little more assurance that this blessing of Abraham is really for you? Then read on a little further in Galatians chapter three. Look at what verse 9 says: "So then they which are of faith are blessed with faithful Abraham" (Gal. 3:9).

Not only are you a child of Abraham, but the Word says here clearly that you are blessed *with* faithful Abraham; in other words, you receive the same blessing He did. As I have given examples of this throughout this book, those who had an encounter with the Spirit of Lord, subsequently had a revelation of Him, His glory and what their inheritance is in Him. He wants to do the same for us today.

My Encounter in January of 2010

Several years ago when I read the last two verses of Galatians chapter three, this truth seemed to jump off the page of my Bible into my heart and I got a clearer revelation of exactly what this blessing of Abraham really is that I've been talking about. It happened during another time of prayer and fasting and while going through my own Abraham-like experience when the Lord brought me into a new season after many years in ministry with Benny Hinn Ministries. Remember I told you earlier, that although I've been a Christian all of my life, been filled with the Holy Spirit at age 12… … graduated with two degrees from two different Bible Colleges … heard countless sermons down through the years, I didn't comprehend this truth fully until a few years ago. However, the Holy Spirit has made it very

real to me and that is why I have not only been com-
pelled to write this book to be able to share it with you,
but I have also preached it around the world and seen
many transformed by its truth and revelation.

Look at what Paul said in Galatians 3:13-14: "Christ
has redeemed us from the curse of the law, having become a curse for us (for it is written, "Cursed is everyone who hangs on a tree.") (vs 14) That the blessing of
Abraham might come upon the Gentiles in Christ Jesus,
that we might receive the promise of the Spirit through
faith" (Gal. 3:13-14).

You Are Blessed!

Verse 13 clearly states that Christ has redeemed us
from the curse of the law. Let's stop right there and establish this fact: if you are a Christian and have been redeemed by the blood of Jesus, you are not cursed! You
are blessed! The blood of Jesus forever lifted the curse
that was introduced into the world through the fall of
Adam and Eve because Jesus, the second Adam, paid
the penalty and price for us to be free of the curse. Regardless of your past, whether you were involved in the
occult, witchcraft or any of the like, no matter what you
have done, or how bad you have been, know that now
that you are in Christ, those demonic spirits no longer
have authority or dominion over you and you are free
from their control by the blood of Jesus! That is why I
can say boldly, you are not cursed, you are blessed!

"That the blessing of Abraham might come on the
Gentiles [that's you and me] through Jesus Christ; the
promise of the Spirit through faith" (Gal. 3:14).

Did you notice that verse 14 begins with the word "that?" That word "that" is a connector between verse 13 and verse 14. In other words, Christ did all that He did in verse 13 (took the curse and penalty of sin and sickness for us) that! That what? Read it again: "that the blessing of Abraham might come on the Gentiles!" Stop! That means you! That means me! Even though we are not Abraham's descendants by blood, we still are his children because of the work of Jesus on the cross is what this verse is saying. That "that" should make you shout out in praise realizing all that is yours as a child of Abraham!

The Promise of The Spirit Through Faith

But Paul goes even further so there would be absolutely no confusion about what the blessing is and defines it in the latter part of verse 14 when he says it's "the promise of the Spirit through faith!" What is the blessing of Abraham? Say it with me, please: "It's the promise of the Spirit through faith!" One more time so that it sinks deep into your spirit: the blessing of Abraham is the promise of the Spirit through faith! It couldn't be any clearer than that but sadly, many of us, including myself, have not fully grasped what the Apostle Paul was trying to tell us here in Galatians. He was trying to tell us that we have as part of our inheritance all of the things I spoke about in the chapters of this book:

The Blessing of Grace
The Blessing of Salvation and Righteousness
The Blessing of Health and Healing
The Blessing of Peace
The Blessing of a Godly Heritage

The Blessing of Faith to Believe for the Impossible
The Blessing of Abundance
The Blessing of Supernatural Intervention
The Blessing of Recovery and Restoration
The Blessing of Divine Protection
The Blessing of Another Spirit
The Blessing of a Heart Transplant

All that I have described in this book about the blessing of Abraham was supernaturally transferred to you and me the moment Jesus died. Hallelujah! It was passed, by the Spirit of Grace, the "hey" of the Spirit through the cross to you and me as believers and we now are recipients of it by faith in Christ Jesus! Wow! What a glorious thought! What a marvelous inheritance is ours!

Remember! The covenant that the Lord God made with Abraham is an eternal covenant which means it will never end. I believe that there is the reason that the Jewish people have become such successful business people, Nobel Prize winners, top scientists, doctors and on and on it goes. What's the reason? It's because of the favor that was on their father Abraham, transferred to his sons and grandchildren and the generations that have followed even until today.

The Holy Spirit Reveals The Blessing in The Word

Most of us who attended Sunday School as a child have heard the story of Noah and the flood. However, I believe it is much more that just a children's story! God became so grieved with the reprobate state of the minds of man that He decided to "wipe the slate clean" as it were and start all over. He found a righteous man named Noah and gave him detailed instructions about building an ark of safety as He was about to destroy the world with a flood in judgment. Noah not only obeyed the word of the Lord and built the Ark exactly according to the blue print God gave him, but he also preached and warned those around him of the impending judgment and gave the call for repentance. Sadly, the lure of their sinful pleasures was greater than their need for God and only Noah's family heeded the warning.

When the ark was completed, Noah made the necessary preparations and systematically organized the loading of the animals followed by his family. When the animals and his family were safely in the ark, the rains began to fall. It rained so much that soon it began to flood and the very ones who had mocked him came screaming desperate cries like "Let us in!" But it was too late; God had sealed the door and the time for repentance was over. God is a patient, loving God, not willing that any should perish; but the Word of God tells us that He will not hold back His judgment forever where sin is concerned.

You know the story ... it rained and rained for forty days and forty nights, and the ark floated up, up, up and carried Noah, his family, and the animals in safety until the rains stopped and the waters subsided.

When the ark was no longer being carried by the waters, it finally came to rest on a place called Mt. Ararat. The word Ararat means "the curse is reversed." A fresh start had been given to man: brand new ground ... a land free from the curse … a land of blessing. What is particularly interesting and I believe symbolically powerful is the fact that it landed on the 17th day of the 7th month of the Hebrew calendar. You might wonder what is significant about that date? Another more important and pivotal event happened in history on the 17th day of the 7th month of the year. Jesus, our Lord and Savior, was crucified and buried in a borrowed tomb on the 14th day of the month. The enemy thought he had won … that he had finally put an end to Him. But, three days later, on the 17th day of the 7th month, Jesus Christ rose victorious over death, hell and the grave in resurrection power. When He did, He became our "heavenly ark" lifting you and me up, up, up to a place of safety, a place of "curse-free ground," and today you and I can boldly say, "the curse is reversed" because Jesus has carried us up to a place of triumph over the curse. Galatians 3:13 says, "Christ has redeemed us from the curse of the law being made a curse for us; for it is written, cursed is every man that hangs on a tree." Every curse of sin, every curse of sickness and disease, poverty and lack, Jesus took on Himself so that you and I could go free and not walk in bondage to sin, shame and sickness but in freedom and victory over sin, and healed in every dimension from the curse. Today we walk on ground that is free from the curse! Hallelujah! That is why I can say with confidence, you are blessed and not cursed! Let me remind you that it was the Holy Spirit that raise Christ from the dead! The word of God says if the Spirit that raised Jesus from the dead is living in us, He will make alive (breathe the Blessing of Abraham) our mortal bodies; that's healing in every dimension of our beings!

The verse says that same miraculous thing that happened to Abram in Genesis 17:5 when God breathed into him the "hey" of His Spirit, quickening (making alive) his dead body, is what happens to us now and is part of our inheritance as Abraham's seed or children.

As I close, I want to share with you some vital keys that I have discovered to releasing and activating the blessing in your life, family, profession or ministry.

Releasing The Blessing

Keys to realizing and releasing the blessing in your life:

1. Stay focused on the Jesus! Matthew 6:33 makes it very clear that if we seek first His Kingdom (seek Him) and make Him central in our hearts and minds and in our lives, "All these things will be added" to us. He's talking about being blessed in all aspects of our lives. #StayFocusedOnJesus

2. Stay in the Word of God! As I have stated, the Word is God-breathed. We literally receive the breath of God (the blessing of Abraham) as we read the Word. Proverbs 4:22 says, "Life and health to all their flesh." #StayInTheWord

3. Stay focused on Him as you read the Word of God! The Bible or the Word of God is not just a book about Him, it IS Him! John said, "In the beginning was the Word and the Word was with God and the Word was God. He is the Word. As you ask the Holy Spirit to reveal Him as you read the Word, He will open up your eyes and show

you Himself from Genesis to Revelations. He will also show you what is yours in Him.
#StayFocusedOnHimAsYourReadTheWord

4. Stay in the Spirit! Those who were in contact with the Holy Spirit in the Bible, in fellowship with Him, received the blessing from the Lord. Like those who were filled on the day of Pentecost in Acts. 2:4, we can experience the "suddenlies" of the Spirit! When you pray, pray often in the Spirit; use the prayer language the Lord has given you and it will breath power and strength into your heart and activate the blessing. #StayInTheSpirit

5. Stay in faith! Faith is like a muscle; the more you exercise it, the more it grows! Dare to believe God for miracles and supernatural intervention! Pray bold prayers for you, your loved ones, your church members, your city and the needs of the world. Call things which do not exist as though they do! (Rom.4:17) Remember! Abraham staggered not at the promise of God…" (Rom. 4:20). Why? Because He had been breathed on by the Holy Spirit, believed God's promise and then stepped out in faith. #StayInFaith #SpeakThoseThingsThatAreNotAsThoughTheyWere

6. Stay expectant! A farmer expects a harvest when he plants a seed in the ground. The God of the harvest will reward you with the fruit and increase of your labors and will transfer the blessing on your life as you give your tithe and sow into good ground above and beyond your tithes. He will prove Malachi 3 to you. #StayExpectant

7. Stay… asking for the blessing! Pray bold prayers like Jabez did in 1 Chronicles 4:10 – "Oh that You would bless me indeed!" God answered His request; He will do the same for you. #AskForTheBlessing

8. Stay abundance minded! Don't focus on your lack or what you do not have. Focus on what you want to see happen in every aspect of your life and pronounce "deshen" (Ps. 65:11) on your life! #StayAbundanceMinded

9. Stay in church, in fellowship with God's people! There is a strength that comes from realizing that we are all part of the body of Christ. Just as one member of the body is affected by what happens in our physical bodies, so we share each others burdens, rejoice with others victories and blessings, receive encouragement from those who are agreeing in faith with us for answered prayer and release of the blessing. #StayInFellowship

10. Stay around people of like faith! Not everyone around you may be at the same level of faith and expectancy that you are for a particular aspect of the blessing. Choose to spend time with those that celebrate your vision, not just tolerate it. Those that agree with the Word, and help to strengthen your faith. Even Jesus had to put out the mourners before He could do the miracle of raising Lazarus! #StayAroundPeopleOfLikeFaith

11. Stay victory minded! You're not a victim; you're a victor. Remember! "Not by might, nor by

power but by My Spirit says the Lord of Hosts!" (Zech. 4:6) #StayVictoryMinded

12. Stay favor minded! Look for and expect miracles in your life because of the blessing. Speak "grace, grace to it!" like the people did in Zechariah 4:6 and see God do for you what He did for Zerubbabel. #StayFavorMinded #StayMiracleMinded

I pray this book has been a blessing and an encouragement to you and that you will truly begin to see the Blessing of Abraham realized in your life in ways you have never imagined!

Why not speak the blessing out of your mouth right now: "I'm blessed with faithful Abraham!" (Gal. 3:9). I believe when you do, you will begin to experience all that this blessing contains. Amen!

For Booking Information:
Call: 949-783-0726
Email: info@certainsoundministries.org

Facebook.com/JimCernero

@JimCernero